DAVID SUTCLIFFE

British Black

English

Basil Blackwell

© David Sutcliffe 1982

First published 1982
Reprinted 1984

Basil Blackwell Limited
108 Cowley Road, Oxford OX4 1JF, England

Basil Blackwell Inc.
432 Park Avenue South, Suite 1505
New York, NY 10016, USA

British Library Cataloguing in Publication Data

Sutcliffe, David
    British black English.
    1. West Indians in Great Britain – Language
    2. Black English – Social aspects
    I. Title
    306   PE3301

    ISBN 0-631-12711-9
    ISBN 0-631-13288-0 Pbk

Typesetting by Unicus Graphics Ltd, Horsham.
Printed in Great Britain.

WITHDRAWN

Contents

For Annjee

Preface

Published at a time when Black people in Britain are daily becoming more aware of their need to assert their cultural independence, *British Black English* must be taken as a series of sketches drawn by an outsider that cannot be complete until they have elicited considerable feedback from the community. However, I hope that educationalists, linguists and lay readers will be able to derive from it some useful information on a complex, intriguing subject.

The book grew out of research carried out since 1973 into the language(s) of Black people in Britain – principally Caribbean- and British-born young people in Bedford. For several years before this I had been teaching in a multiracial school and learning at first hand how West Indian pupils fare in British education. The Bedford Survey mentioned in the text is a rather grand label for research carried out for an M. Ed. degree while I was on secondment from Bedfordshire Education Authority. In the course of this research, I gathered and analysed taped speech-data and data from questionnaires and informal discussion. Since then I have completed a study of British Black oral narrative, funded by the Social Science Research Council and based at the Institute of Education, London, under the guidance of Professor Harold Rosen. This stock of experience has been supplemented by the distinctively Black plays, poems, essays and short stories that I have read, studied, and above all enjoyed. At the same time I have learnt a great deal, informally, from many Black friends.

In part I, after an introductory consideration of Creoles as valid languages, and discussion of their possible processes of formation, the interaction between language and culture is explored through the rich range of Black oral and written literature. Jennifer Johnson's lively short story in London Jamaican and Neville Moore's discussion of the Rastafarian movement in Bedford are included in this part. The education chapter provides a concise summary of the main issues and incorporates John Richmond's valuable insights into classroom practice.

Part II deals with theoretical linguistic aspects in more detail, including the operation of the continuum (of language varieties between Creole and English) and the rationale behind dialect selection. However, there is also directly applicable information on the grammar (in chapter 4) and lexis (in the Glossary).

My objective, in the book, has been to show British Black language and culture not as subcultural nor makeshift, but as the creative development of an Afro-American tradition in a new environment, integrated, complex and distinctive, despite constant adaptation. There has been a long history of underestimating or ignoring Black language. When distinctively Black speech *is* noticed it is often labelled 'political'. In fact Creoles have always been languages of resistance and declarations of Black independence. But it seems to me that the primary reasons for talking Black in Britain are joy in the language itself and satisfaction in being one's self.

Recent events in Britain have drawn attention to the frustrations of inner city life, and the problems which Black pupils have in British schools. It is good that these matters have come into the open at last. But there is a real danger that the British public will continue to see West Indians as actually *being* the problem. Also the whole concept of problem induces a self-fulfilling and self-perpetuating negativity. Black people in Britain have potential that will out whatever national governments or white majorities do. And in the field of education, for example, it can be seen that quite simple (inexpensive) moves on the part of the school can bring pupils back into a trusting relationship with their teachers, and bring out the particular cultural strengths that are there.

A few words on terminology may be appropriate here. 'Patois' and 'Creole' are used interchangeably to refer to the highly non-standard forms of speech current in the Caribbean and Guyana, and their British extensions. 'Black', 'West Indian' and 'Caribbean' are used more or less interchangeably to describe both people and things Caribbean and Guyanese, and their British continuations – the second and third generation of Black people in Britain and their culture. These latter are, of course, British Black people rather than Black British, so the title of this book is to be read *(British) Black English*. It is perhaps pertinent to note at this point that for me and for many Black people the term 'Black' has primarily a cultural reference (though the racial dimension has had a dramatic effect on the culture). Thus members of the Black community can, in my view, be of any colour including white. For this reason alone the word Black is used with a capital letter.

Acknowledgements

My first thanks go to Jennifer Johnson, Neville Moore (of the Bedford Caribbean Youth Association) and John Richmond for making their work available for publication within this volume. Jennifer Johnson's *Ballad For You* was first published in *Race Today* in January 1978. A fuller version of John Richmond's piece was published as 'Dialect in the Classroom' in *The English Magazine* (ILEA English Centre, Sutherland Street, London SW1) in 1979. Neville Moore's piece has not previously been published.

Secondly, I should like to thank all the young West Indians in Bedford and Luton who participated in the research. Their names all have been altered in the text but this was a very hard decision to make, balancing the slightly greater need for confidentiality against the desire to give credit where it was due. Of all the adult Black Bedfordians who have helped me, I especially thank Mrs Carter and family, Pastor Vaughn of the Miracle Church of God and Christ, Mrs Ayton and Neville Moore.

For encouragement at the beginning I would like to thank Brian Harrison and my then headmaster Mr Brian Hodgson; also the other head teachers of Bedford schools who assisted me, especially Mrs Herbert and Mr Hubbard, and Mr Swan and Mr Alsop of Challney High School for Boys in Luton. I am especially grateful for helpful comments on the draft chapters from Tony Burgess, Viv Edwards, Rosemary Joyeux, Billy Nawathe, John Richmond, Delroy Salmon, Sheila Sloan and Rosemary Thomas. At a very late stage Marcia Smith and Doreen Brown rendered invaluable assistance in checking lexical entries. Any remaining defects are, of course, my responsibility alone. Rick Collet and his colleagues at the Bedford Resources Centre provided unstinting and valuable support. Professor Harold Rosen also provided indispensable support for which I shall always be indebted. My thanks go to Shirley Hadi for her very helpful insights and information, to Dr Pauline Christie of the University of the West Indies, who very kindly wrote to me providing her observations on the language of *Ballad For You* and other Black British texts, and also to Ansel Wong of the Elimu Centre, London, for his timely help. Mr Harshud Vyas and family also gave valuable support of a different kind at one point of the work. Above all I wish to thank Dr Peter Trudgill for his assistance and encouragement over several years. My thanks lastly go to the staff of Bedford Library especially Mrs Polly Elder, and to Mrs West, Mrs MacDonald and Mrs Wiser for typing the manuscript.

The debt I owe to my family is more than I can easily acknowledge.

Spelling Conventions

Because Jamaican Creole (JC) can be viewed as a different language from English, and tends to be viewed as such by its speakers (at least in Britain), it merits a spelling convention of its own. So far, however, writers who use the Creole have not arrived at one consistent convention, and this difficulty is reflected in the varying styles of orthography used in this book. The main possibilities are:

(1) The use of English spellings wherever possible. Only words that are not English in immediate origin are spelt according to JC pronunciation. See, for instance, 'The Big Aunty Katie', in the Texts section at the end of the book.

(2) Use of a more modified English orthography. Wherever consonantal pronunciations are non-English these are indicated. Function words (often ambiguously English/non-English) are spelt according to pronunciation using an orthography similar to (4) below. Such words include **se(h)**, **fi**, **di**, **dem** (plural marker), the personal pronouns and the demonstratives. This is the method most commonly used in this book.

(3) An orthography still more modified from the conventional English style, where certain Creole vowel values are indicated throughout:

> drap (drop)
> gaan (gone)

and perhaps:

> straa (straw) versus
> floor or flo (floor)

(4) Finally there is the completely non-English orthography, originally devised by the authors of the *Dictionary of Jamaican English* (Cassidy and Le Page 1967) for their Creole entries (this orthography has subsequently been used by linguists when transcribing Creoles, adapting it where necessary). In this phonemic convention all words are indicated consistently according to the systematic spelling rules – this means that even words like 'school' and 'pick', which are pronounced virtually as in standard English, are spelt *skuul* and *pik*. All JC entries set in italics in this book are spelt according to this orthography.

This list does not exhaust the possibilities, of course. *Ballad For You* (pp. 24–31) is perhaps more impressionistically spelt, in a style varying between (2) and (3). O'Connor's *Jamaica Child* (pp. 61–2) also settles on a style between (2) and (3), but tends to have **me** rather than Creole **mi** (though not **you** for Creole **yu**) and also **de** (di), **fe** (fi) and so on.

Another possibility for divergence is choice of the exact method for writing the distinctive word-final short back vowels:

> so, soh, or suh   /sɔ/
> no, noh, or nuh   /nɔ/
> du, duh (or even 'dhu' in *BFY*)   /du/ for English 'do'
> yu or yuh   /ju/

Further problems arise in the spelling of language that is either variable between Creole and less broad speech, or consistently less than broad Creole (mesolect). Note in this connection that style (4) cannot be mixed with the other spelling conventions without indicating change of convention by means of type face (etc.). When transcribing language that shows slight but noticeable variation (very common indeed, at least in British Jamaican Creole), the transcriber has to choose between deciding what the overall choice of dialect is in a passage and ignoring the minor fluctuations in pronunciation (at least where they do not indicate some sort of lexical or grammatical difference), or alternatively indicating every fluctuation that the spelling convention can register. A fuller discussion of this topic of spelling is to be found in Le Page (1972).

Writers who set out to write in Creole (not to transcribe speech) have a decided advantage in that (having adopted a convention) they can monitor variation in their language according to their needs (that is, reduce it to what they feel is significant or appropriate).

PART I

Culture and Society

CHAPTER 1

Introduction

The birth of a new speech variety is the kind of linguistic event that used to go unnoticed or at least undocumented until years after it happened. Because of seventeenth- and early eighteenth-century prejudices against non-standard dialect and 'uncivilized' society, it is difficult to say now, at this distance, what the earliest Caribbean Creoles were like when they first began to be spoken alongside the African languages, or even exactly what went into their formation. In the case of the transmission of distinctive Black speech from the Caribbean to England, however, we have the opportunity to observe linguistic change and linguistic history at first hand. We can make tape recordings of the different age groups and ask questions of the people involved. We also have an opportunity to observe what happens to a highly non-standard dialect when most of its speakers become proficient in a more standard form of English. (It is difficult to differentiate between a language and a dialect on linguistic criteria; here dialect is used to stress the connection with standard English.)

This area of inquiry must hold considerable appeal to anyone with a theoretical interest in language. There are also practical implications for teachers, educational policy-makers, sociologists, indeed anyone with a practical interest in Britain's multicultural society. Teachers in modern Britain, for example, need to know about the emergent British Black speech and the Caribbean language and cultural background from which it has sprung – otherwise this Black language will remain a reinforcement of the divide in society rather than a bridge leading to real understanding.

There have, of course, been Black people living in Britain since Saxon times and probably earlier, and by the sixteenth century there were sufficient numbers here to cause concern to Elizabeth I. In 1596 she issued an edict seeking to limit the immigration of 'blackamoors' into England (Acts of the Privy Council 26, 1596–7, p. 16). In more recent times Black communities have grown up in seaport cities such as Cardiff and Liverpool and have now been there for some four or five generations. After the Second World War, however, much larger numbers of emigrants left the Caribbean to settle in urban centres and obtain employment in those areas of industry where there was at the time an acute shortage of labour. This usually meant taking menial, unattractive jobs, often on low pay. A survey carried out in 1958–59 showed that 55 per cent of Black migrants accepted jobs of lower status than those held in the country of origin. The hope of the first generation of settlers was that their children would do better, and would be able to move up from this low rung on the socioeconomic ladder after receiving a British education. Unfortunately the English-born generation feels trapped in this lowly position in society and unable to escape except in individual cases. For a whole complex of reasons, having much to do with discrimination (directly or indirectly), the rate of unemployment among Black youths is four times higher than among the population as a whole. Two opposing strategies open to young Black people in this situation are: assume that prejudice will eventually be overcome, accept the values of the host society and take on its life-style, becoming Black Britons in every sense; or reject mainstream society (or at least its values) and turn to an emphatically Black life-style, fostering a distinct Black, non-European identity. Individual Blacks have chosen one course or the other, but the community as a whole is probably choosing to do what Afro-American communities have almost always done to a lesser or greater extent: maintain a dual identity involving a set of white behaviours and an 'Afro' set. These sets include ways of worshipping, celebrating and having fun, music,[1] food and dress, ways of moving, eye behaviours, ways

---

[1] On the subject of music and dancing, whites have been heavily influenced by Blacks, so the divergence here is not as great as it used to be.

of joking, laughing and conducting conversations, of censuring or manipulating others, and – of special interest here – forms of dialect. Black communities in Britain are maintaining the whole range of language from the local English variety through to strikingly unEnglish Black speech derived from Caribbean Creoles.

This simple fact underpins a complex linguistic situation. Firstly, before one considers a spread of dialect brought about by having Creole-speaking parents and white playmates, it is well to remember that language in, say, Jamaica ranges from examples such as *im fi kaal im breda*, through *shi tu kaal im broda* to 'she's to call him brother', which in British English would be 'he's her brother' or 'she's his sister' – so the original range of dialect was already very great. Secondly, although about 60 per cent of Black migrants are from Jamaica, there are also considerable numbers from other islands and territories including Trinidad, Guyana, Barbados and the Windward and Leeward Islands, and these people speak varieties that, although largely sharing an underlying grammar with Jamaican Creole, can be rather different in terms of vocabulary, idiom and pronunciation. (Bajan – Barbadian – is probably the variety that differs most from Jamaican, while the Creoles of the Leeward Islands and of St Vincent are considerably less different.) As Le Page (1972) suggests, with particular reference to his Jamaican, Grenadian and St Vincentian texts, they are in essence different dialects of the same West Indian Creole language. It must also not be overlooked that many St Lucians and Dominicans and even some Trinidadians and Grenadians have French-based Creoles as well as English-based varieties in their speech repertoire. Thirdly, there is the factor of geographic separation in this country to consider. The centres of Black population are islands of Black speech in a white sea – though not so cut off from one another as one might suppose. Such diverse mixes of speech might be expected to produce different linguistic results in different speech communities. Again, while this must be so, the differences, particularly in terms of straightforward grammar and pronunciation, are probably slighter than one might at first suspect. The subject of this book then is a dynamic language situation reflecting an equally dynamic cultural situation, which, although new to this country, is the continuation of a meeting – or clashing – of cultures that has been going on for hundreds of years.

A SYSTEMATIC LANGUAGE

It is all too easy to regard English Creoles as a distortion or perversion of English, hotchpotches of non-standard forms with no rules. It is true that Jamaican Creole (JC), for instance, exhibits a fluctuation of grammatical forms to an extent not found in standard English (SE). In *Ballad For You* (*BFY*), the London Jamaican story at the end of this chapter, Jennifer Johnson sometimes writes **she** (for all cases) and sometimes **her**:

> Di addah gal dem all bundle roun' **she** fi fill **her** in
> pan di situation.

– while the classic form for this personal pronoun in broad JC is neither **shi** nor **her** but **im**, the same pronoun covering male and female gender:

> ***im** beli big.*
> (She is pregnant.)

British-born Black people seem to use this feminine **im** only occasionally, probably for special effect (in the above it shows derision), but in straight linguistic terms they have a choice between /im/, /shi/ and /har/ even when speaking in their broadest style. They also have a choice for the first person singular subject pronoun between /mi/, /a/ and /ai/, and the same holds true for a number of other constantly recurring features. This kind of fluctuation is caused by interplay with standard English. In the same way, most Londoners sometimes pronounce the /h/ sound in words like High Holborn and sometimes not, because of the interplay between Cockney and 'educated' English pronunciation. However, the fluctuation or 'linguistic variation' found in all the Atlantic Creole languages (Caribbean, American and West African Creoles) coexisting with European standards does seem to be of a different order. I shall return to this point in chapter 3.

Actually the language of *Ballad For You* is highly consistent in many ways, as we shall see, and the variation is largely superficial. It is not 'wrong' in any case, but simply an integral part of the living language and a reflection of the social pressures bearing on it and its speakers. There have always been forces on JC that would decreolize it – that is, cause it to evolve toward standard English – largely held in check by opposite forces of recreolization: social or psychological trends that assert the 'creoleness' of Creole.

A second reason why English Creoles are often dismissed as debased lies in their very resemblance to English. From the standpoint of standard English,

> Ain't you is a hag?
> (You're a witch, aren't you?)

constitutes an aberration of syntax (Turner 1949: 279). However, from a Creole standpoint this sentence, culled from Gullah (an American cousin of JC), is well formed.[2] Similarly in *Ballad For You*

> ... You **aint** know anybody.

is odd 'English' but features **aint** or /ɛ̃/ in its Creole role as negative marker, a variant of broad Creole **no**. If we wish to understand and appreciate Creoles fully we must try to view them as languages working according to their own rules, and grammatically different from English even when seeming to resemble English fairly closely. To take a JC example (Bailey 1966: 65):

> The baby name Robert.

Any English speaker in tune with Jamaican pronunciation would understand what this meant even if it was said: **di biebi niem Rabat**. What he could not do, without some knowledge of JC, would be to appreciate its grammaticality. He would take it to be English with 'pieces missing', either:

> The baby (is) name(d) Robert.

---

[2] Compare the use of **aint** /ɛ̃/ in San Andres Creole (J. Edwards, Rosberg and Prime Hoy (1975: 297, 298).

or, more probably:

The baby('s) name (is) Robert.

Either assumption would normally be wrong, and cause him to view the syntax as defective or 'babyish'. Here **niem** is a verb equivalent to French 's'appeler' (to be called); in other words it is reflexive in meaning. It can be given tense just as other verbs can, but here in its unmarked form it refers to the present state of affairs. All Caribbean Creoles have this and many other constructions that are not English in origin, but that arguably derive in the first place from West African pidgin English. So paradoxically, while it is necessary to be able to view JC and other Atlantic Creoles as languages in their own right separate from English, one way to do this is to compare these Creoles with each other, with African Pidgin and even indigenous African languages.

LANGUAGE SIMPLIFICATION OR 'RATIONALIZATION'

Creoles and Pidgins are said to have undergone simplification, which in this sense really amounts to rationalization – a shedding of 'redundant' word endings and irregular verbs – rather than any real reduction in the power or subtlety of the language.

Of course English, too, has been simplified from its old English form, and for basically the same reason: after the Viking and Norman invasions the Norse speakers and French speakers in effect pidginized and creolized the language, causing nearly all redundant inflections to be dropped. Such a process does not entail the loss of grammatical distinctions such as those expressed by a developed verb system – we would properly resent any such accusation of grammatical bluntness levelled at English. This can be well illustrated by comparing the verb system of a highly inflected language such as Latin with that of an Atlantic Creole.

The Surinam Creole, Sranan, has three basic pre-verbal markers **ben**, **sa** and **e**. Through permutation of these, the Creole's eight different tenses – or, more accurately, tense-aspect forms of the verb – are expressed (see figure 1.1).

FIGURE 1.1 *Sranan pre-verbal markers*

		past	present	
	realis	ben-	(zero)	*completive*
MODE	*non-realis*	ben-sa-	sa	
	realis	ben-e-	e-	
	non-realis	ben-sa-e-	sa-e	*non completive*

And at the right: ASPECT

Source: Voorhoeve (1962: 39).

These forms are placed before the verb like this: **mi ben-lobi en** ('I loved him'). The terms that the linguist uses to describe the language are unfamiliar. 'Non-completive' here means progressive or habitual; 'non-realis' means conditional. The point is that Sranan is capable of expressing with three small words and a set of personal pronouns the same number of tenses that it takes Latin some 192 different verb forms to express. That is, another 180 forms like:

amo	amabam
amas	amabas
amat	amabat
amamus	amabamus
amatis	amabatis
amant	amabant

Latin has a battery of inflections for nouns, pronouns, adjectives and demonstratives. English has very largely discarded these inflections. Jamaican Creole, Sranan and the other Atlantic Creoles have completely done so while retaining a range of 'necessary' (that is non-redundant) grammatical distinctions, expressed by auxiliary verbs, prefixes and suffixes.

RESTRICTED AND ELABORATED LANGUAGE, AND JAMAICAN CREOLE

Much has been written about the tendency of middle-class people towards using elaborated English and the tendency of working-class speakers towards using unelaborated English. This observation is related to and easily confused with other issues such as the relationship between speech and writing and the maturational process of language development. Elaboration is a nebulous concept. Basically it is used to refer to the complexity of the syntax and the amount and variety of adjectives and adverbs in a given piece of language. According to Basil Bernstein, whose work on this subject has had enormous influence in educational circles, elaborated language (or code) bears the stamp of the speaker's individuality and is 'context-independent'.

To avoid too much elaboration ourselves, let us focus as sharply as possible on perhaps the most important consideration: syntactic elaboration. Elaboration or complexity of syntax (sentence structure) is merely a dimension: syntax is more or less elaborated. Although the expression of complex ideas frequently leads a speaker to use more complicated syntax, there is no fixed relationship between the two. Furthermore, elaboration is not the only yardstick that can be used to describe language on what we might call the stylistic level or what linguists call the discourse level. It may not even be the most important one. At the risk of reducing the argument to the absurd the reader is invited to compare the following two passages:

> It's raining, it's pouring,
> The old man's snoring,
> He went to bed and bumped his head,
> And couldn't get up in the morning.

> Thus I; faltering forward
> Leaves around me falling
> Wind oozing thin through the thorn from norward
> And the woman calling.

'It's raining, it's pouring' is, of course, a well-known children's rhyme. The second item, which has a similar unelaborated sentence structure, is the climax to Thomas Hardy's poem 'The voice'. Of course there is a world of difference between the two that hardly registers on a scale of elaboration. For very different reasons their plain structure is suited to their purposes. It is clearly a sterile procedure to consider elaboration separate from function. Situation, the 'genre' and the choice of medium all have their effect in this respect. In our writing we all tend to use longer, more complicated sentences than if we are talking, because we have the leisure to read back, consider, cross out or even begin again, and we know that our readers can likewise take their time in absorbing our message. The quotation below is a 'literal' translation of the entry for 787 in the *Old English Chronicle*. It is in an unelaborated style, heavily dependent on simple coordination – the use of conjunctions like 'and' – probably because it was written in the vernacular of the time, which was very much a spoken rather than written language:

Here King Beorhtric took King Offa's daughter Eardburg. And in his day first came three ships; and the reeve rode there, and he wanted to drive them to the King's town, because he did not know what they were; and they killed him. Those were the first Danish ships that sought England.

Actual elaboration, then, depends on a variety of contextual factors.

A speaker's potential or capacity for elaboration is another matter. This depends on the speaker/writer's maturity – not just his or her age but the amount of exposure to various more or less elaborated styles of language including a range of written styles. The ability to build complex sentences, using a variety of different types of clauses subordinated to a main clause, only comes with age and experience. I have suggested that this ability is exercised in writing rather than speech, but (as we shall see later) adept speakers who feel compelled to communicate a complex idea quickly can often exhibit quite complicated syntax, although 'thinking on their feet'. They may hesitate, stop and reformulate, but that is just the oral equivalent of deletions and omission marks. Some Black speakers I have recorded do not even do that when under pressure to perform fluently. *Ballad For You* appears to be a writing down of this kind of oral performance. William Labov in his study of narrative syntax noted a particular stylistic device used by only the most mature narrators in his sample, and which he labelled 'left-hand embedding'. This involves complication of the noun phrase before the verb. *BFY* shows various types of syntactic complexity, including left-hand embedding:

> One by one **di man whey chalice dida dance wid woman an she fren dem** a tip-toe outside.
> (One by one the-man-whom-Chalice-had-been-dancing-with's woman and her friends were tip-toeing outside.)

This comprises a grammatical subject of twelve words dominating a predicate of six and manages to be both compressed and elaborated language at the same time. It is also exactly the sort of speech that some have labelled 'restricted ghetto language'.

THE EMERGENCE OF ATLANTIC CREOLES

Jamaican speech and Jamaican life-styles have been shaped by a culture clash that has been going on for hundreds of years. It would be useful at this point to trace the early history and development of the language since pre-slavery days. Despite sparse documentation on the critical formative period between, say, 1650 and 1725, we can gather something of what happened by the use of comparative linguistics – the comparison of languages.

Before the fifteenth century West Africans were relatively free from European interference. A large proportion of the population were, and still are, multilingual. The reason for this is clear when you consider that of the 400 or so languages mapped for the area by David Dalby (1977) few have more than one million speakers. Dalby has this to say of West African languages and their speakers.

Divergences in their structures, i.e. in their grammatical, phonological and semantic systems, are frequently less extensive than their divergences of vocabulary, and – relative to the structures of European languages – West African languages are found to share many widespread structural features. As a result, Africans are often well experienced in operating divergent sets of vocabulary, as they master a variety of different languages, but in doing so are able to maintain many of the grammatical, phonological and semantic rules which they have acquired as part of their original mother tongue. [Dalby 1970: 6]

This switching between languages is made easier by the grammatical and other similarities. At the same time, the similarities themselves may have been brought about, or at least maintained, by the language switching. The linguist John Gumperz has shown how languages 'converge' on one another – become more alike – when they are used daily in a multilingual situation, as they have been in Kupwar, India, for some 600 years.

During the fifteenth and sixteenth centuries Europeans made increasing contact with the peoples living along the coast of West Africa, to trade manufactured goods for slaves and raw materials. Consequently, more and more West Africans turned to a European language, at first Portuguese and later English or French, as lingua franca (common language used for inter-group communication). When Africans spoke these languages, African idiom and varieties of pronunciation were carried over. The grammars were completely recast so that they had few structures in common with the original European tongues, and the inflections disappeared almost completely. In this way new varieties of speech were created – new African languages known to linguists and laymen as Pidgins. They have little in common with their so-called European models. It is possible, however, to demonstrate that at least some of their characteristic structural features have parallels in West African languages.

In the sixteenth century, slave ships began to transport African slaves to the Americas. The Pidgins were transported with them, and it is arguable that these became the basis for all the Creoles in the New World. The accepted definition of a Creole is a Pidgin that has become a mother tongue. Recent evidence suggests that these Pidgin/Creoles became in a sense the adopted mother tongues of the African slaves within a very few years or even months of their arrival on the plantations (cf. Price 1976: 21–2).

THE SPREAD OF PIDGIN/CREOLE VOCABULARY

Amongst other privations, the early slaves had an extreme language problem to overcome. They urgently needed a common language. They probably soon learnt to understand the few short commands, warnings, and other stock phrases which they would hear from the overseer. This would not in any way have amounted to learning the white language even in 'broken' form. In some regions white artisans, indentured labourers, and poor white settlers might have provided a richer source of language or at least *words*. Words were the most immediate need, lexical tokens that could be used with whatever grammar (provided there was an agreement on the most fundamental word orders). West African Pidgins were of prime importance in this respect. The pattern everywhere seems to have been that Africans who had a knowledge of the Pidgin equivalent to the plantation owners' language became transmitters of a new vocabulary that disseminated throughout the plantation. We can be reasonably certain of the importance of West African Pidgins because of the core of distinctive vocabulary shared by many different Creoles.

Some of the common items for English-based Creoles are shown in table 1.1. They are derived from (regional) English, and various African languages. The most likely explanation for their widespread occurrence is that they were carried

TABLE 1.1 *Common, distinctive vocabulary across four English Creoles*

English	JC	Sranan	Saramaccan	Gullah
because	bika, ka	bikási	bigá	ka
boa con-				
strictor	–	aboma	boma	bɔma*
breast	bobi	bɔbi	bɔbi	–
bring	kya, kyari	tya, kya	tya	tya
eat	nyam	nyám	nyām	yam, nyam
greedy	bigai, bigyai	bigai	–	bigɔi
if	ef, if	efu	e(f)i	ef, if
scattered	wanwan	wawan	wanwán	βáβan (wanwan)
			(= sole)	
whiteman	bakra	bakra	bakáa	bʌkrə
you (pl.)	unu	unu	ún, únù	unə

* 'a large brownish snake' (Turner 1949: 191). Turner offers Kikongo (the black python) as an etymology.

in a Pidgin that originated in Africa. There are also pronunciation features common to almost all English-based Atlantic Creoles: the substitution of /b/ for English /v/, and of /t/ and /d/ for English /θ/ and /ð/ as in thing and leather. The 'simplifying' of clusters of consonants at the beginning of words is another common feature. Interestingly, French Creoles also show a common core of vocabulary. Table 1.2 illustrates this very well.

TABLE 1.2 *Common, distinctive vocabulary across five French Creoles*

French	Haiti	Lesser Antilles	French Guyana	Louisiana	Indian Ocean
oiseau (bird)	zozo zwazo zwezo zhwazo	zozo zwazo	zozo	zozo zwazo	zozo zwazo
oeuil (eye)	zhe, zye	zye	wey	ze, zye	lezye
maison (house)	kaz, kay lakay	kaz, kay lakay	kaz	mezõ	lakaz
personne (person)	mun	mun	mun	mun	mun, dimun
eau (water)	dlo, dyo gyo, glo	dlo, dyo gyo, glo	dilo	dolo	dilo
avoir (have)	gẽnye, gẽ	gẽnye/tini	gẽnye	gẽnye/ ena/yena	ganye
donner (give)	bay	bay	bay	done	done
savoir (know)	kõnẽ	konɛt, sav	konɛt, save	konẽ	konẽ
tenir (hold)	kẽbe	kyẽbe, tshẽbe	kyene, tshẽbe	tshõmbo	tshõmbo
tirer (pull)	rale	rale, hale	rale	hale	hale/ale

Source: Adapted from Valdman 1978: 13.

Cruikshank (1916) provides us with an account of language learning by a newly arrived African. It is very late,
taken down by Cruikshank from 'an old African in Demarara'
in the earlier part of this century, but it could well illustrate
the process in the crucially important formative years:

'You know no English at all when you come to Bakra Country?'
'T all 't all!'
'Who teach you when you come?'
'Who l'arn me? Eh-eh! No me matty?'
'How he learn you? Gi'e you book and so?'
'Book! Youse'f too! A-we nation got book? Fo' a-we book yah!'

He touched his chest, where the Negro 'mind' is supposed to reside;
his memory was his book.

'What fashion you learn?'
'Da Uncle me a lib wit' he se'f l'arn me. Uncle a say, "Bwoy, tekky
dis crabash [calabash] – de crabash dey a he hand – go dip watah.
Watah-watah da ting inside da barrel, O." So Uncle do, sotay me a
ketch wan-wan Engreesh.'
'So all of you catch Bakra talk, little by little?'
'Ah! Same thing! Matty a l'arn matty, matty a l'arn matty. You no
see da fashion pickny a l'arn fo' talk – when he papa a talk he a watch
he papa mout'?'

['You didn't know any English at all when you came to the white
man's country?'
'None at all!'
'Who taught you when you came?'
'Who taught me? Eh-eh! Who else but my friend?'
'How did he teach you? Did he give you a book and so on?'
'Book! You gotta be kiddin'! Does our people have books? Our
books are here!' ...
'In what manner did you learn?'
'It was Uncle whom I lived with who taught me himself. Uncle
would say "Boy, take this calabash – the calabash would be in his
hand – and go dip water. Water-water, the thing inside the barrel."
So Uncle did, until I picked up English little by little.'
'So you all picked up white man's talk, little by little?'
'Yes, that's it. A friend would teach a friend, that friend would be
teaching another friend. Haven't you ever seen how a child learns to
talk – when his father is talking he'll be watching his father's mouth?']

FORMATION OF THE GRAMMAR

As the common vocabulary spread from 'matty' to 'matty' in chain reaction fashion the grammatical structures of a new language were being evolved. Strategically the first step was to agree on a subject-verb-object (SVO) word order as the basic pattern. This order is common to English, French, Portuguese, Spanish, West African English Pidgin and a great many of the relevant African languages. (French and other Romance languages have SVO order when the object is a noun: Jean aime Marie, but SOV order when the object takes the form of a personal pronoun: Jean l'aime. French Creoles have SVO order in either instance.) The placement of the adjective (or other modifier) before or after the noun had also to be agreed upon. English Creoles generally place the modifier before the modified. This is in contradistinction to many African languages, notably those most likely to be involved, and in accord with English and West African Pidgin. These two basic features of word order make for the (frequently misleading) match between English and English Creoles that I have already mentioned.

From this point onward the new language would have expanded and complexified quite swiftly. The speakers would have drawn on their own collective resources, learning from each other in countless verbal interactions: grumbling, cussing, retailing anecdotes and old stories, joking, moralizing, plotting and planning. At the same time they were piecing together a new Afro-American identity in which the language came to be deeply enmeshed. Dalby's observation on African multilingualism suggests that these first speakers would have attempted to carry over the grammatical structures of their mother tongue and other African languages. Linguists are divided as to whether such attempts were successful, in view of the enormous number of mother tongues involved. There is no doubt that African-derived structural features *did* survive. However, some linguists consider these to be relatively unimportant, and stress instead the way in which competing features must have clashed. This, they argue, must have resulted in the creation of an essentially new grammatical system, deriving its form from universal principles of language. Some linguists also believe that processes of language simplification were important. As we have seen, their effects were perhaps largely confined to the surface detail of Creole languages.

On the question of the speed with which the new languages formed and the comparative lack of reference to the masters' languages in the process, support is to be found in the intriguing language history of Surinam. I have already mentioned Sranan, the English-based Creole that is the mother tongue of the majority of Surinamers, akin to Jamaican Creole though not readily intelligible to JC speakers. Also spoken in the forested interior is the part-Portuguese, part-English based Saramaccan spoken by descendants of Africans who escaped from the plantations around the turn of the eighteenth century. There are other groups in the interior, descended from Africans who escaped at a later date, and they speak varieties of Ndjuka, an English-based Creole, which is partly intelligible to Sranan speakers.

Serious English settlement and exploitation of the territory began in 1650. In 1667 the territory was ceded to the Netherlands in exchange for New Amsterdam (renamed New York). After this date there was an overlap period of some five years during which the slaves of the English and Dutch were together in Surinam. Then the English planters and their slaves departed. Despite the shortness of the overlap period, Surinamers have, amazingly, continued to speak Sranan rather than a creolized version of Dutch. This suggests that Proto-Sranan formed rapidly, with little reference to the master's language after the very earliest stage. In Jamaica, too, there is a polarization between Creole and English, although there is also much use of intermediate language, Creole-like in structure but approximating more nearly to English in its surface forms – thus the distinction between the opposing languages is blurred.

If the first Sranan speakers' contact with 'English' was fleeting, the first Saramaccan speakers' contact with any kind of plantation culture or language was equally fleeting. It is estimated that virtually all the ancestral Saramaccans who escaped into the forests had been in Surinam for less than ten years when they did so (Price 1976: 32). Yet they too evolved a Creole language with a largely European vocabulary base. Saramaccan has tone as the African languages do, and in general seems suitably non-European, but its grammatical structure and semantics resemble those of JC and other geographically distant Creoles evolved by Africans who stayed in the plantations (because there was nowhere for them to escape to).

Whatever the differences between the early linguistic histories of Jamaica and Surinam, there are demonstrable similarities in the end result, suggesting that linguistic processes, and perhaps the psychology underlying them, were similar. Compare Sranan and JC in the following passage adapted from Voorhoeve (1962). The translation into JC is idiomatic (with one small exception), and yet matches the original word by word *and* construction by construction (the English version is included for clarification):

Sr: Dem sma taki: mi no e-leri i ibri dey
JC: *Dem smadi se: mi no laan yu ebri die*
   (Them somebody say: I not teach you everyday)

Sr: taki yu mus kon a oso, yu mus kon nyan
JC: *se yu mos kom a yaad, yu mos kom nyam*
   (say you must come at home, you must come eat)

Sr: fos yu go go prey. En dat wroko
JC: *bifuo yu go go plie. An dat wok*
   (before you go go play. And that work)

Sr: de a oso fu du. Dan yu e-go go, taki
JC: *de a yaad fi du. Den yu a-go go, se*
   (is at home for do. Then you are going go, say)

Sr: yu e-go sywen. We mi e-go sywen
JC: *yu a-go swim. Wel mi a-go swim*
   (you are going swim. Well I am going swim)

Sr: yu futu gi yu.
JC: *yu fut gi yu.*
   (your leg give you (i.e. for you).)

THE EARLY USE OF ENGLISH

Besides Pidgin/Creole, African languages and European languages were spoken in these early days particularly perhaps by those who disassociated themselves from the pan-African spirit of the plantation.

It has often been pointed out that the Blacks who worked or even lived in the master's house learnt the master's language, or something close to it. This must have been true even of some African born. An outstanding example to set against Cruikshank's 'Old African' is the poet Phillis Wheatley. She is thought to have been born in Senegal somewhere around 1753, was enslaved and shipped to America and was bought by John Wheatley, tailor of Boston, in 1761 (cf. Wagner 1973). After sixteen months she knew English so well that she could 'read any, the most difficult parts of the sacred writings' (letter from John Wheatley to Phillis's London publisher, 14 November 1772). By the age of 16 she could read Virgil and Horace in the original. She began to write poetry (in English) extolling Christianity – and also protesting against the tyranny of slavery, as in these lines addressed to William, Earl of Dartmouth, on his appointment as Secretary for North America:

> Should you, my lord, while you peruse my song,
> Wonder from whence my love of Freedom sprung,
> Whence flow these wishes for the common good,
> By feeling hearts alone best understood;
> I, young in life, by seeming cruel fate
> Was snatch'd from Afric's fancy'd happy seat;
> What pangs excruciating must molest,
> What sorrows labor in my parent's breast?
> Steel'd was that soul and by no misery mov'd
> That from a father seiz'd his babe belov'd;
> Such, such my case. And can I then but pray
> Others may never feel tyrannic sway?

EARLIER STAGES OF JAMAICAN CREOLE

It has proved difficult to find examples of Jamaican Creole preserved in writing that pre-date 1790, but from this time onward there is increasingly abundant evidence of a Jamaican Creole virtually identical to the modern variety and no broader than the modern extreme. Moreton wrote down the following song in 1790. It was supposedly sung by a slave as she danced (**wind** rhymes **bind**):

> Hipsaw! my deaa! You no shake like a-me!
> You no wind like a-me!
> Hipsaw! My deaa! You no do like a-me!
> You no jig like a-me! You no twist like a-me!
> Hipsaw! my deaa! ...
>
> [Cassidy 1961: 272]

Cassidy explains that Hipsaw was a kind of dance in which the hips oscillated back and forth, whereas **wind** 'was the early word for twisting and turning the hips'. Actually **wind** is still very much alive and in use in modern Jamaican:

> Who dat bwoy over dear **ah-whine-in** himself. Mussi
> tink him a something big. ['Jamaican Story' –
> a play written by girls at Vauxhall Manor
> School, London]
> (Who's that boy over there **wind**ing himself? Must
> think he's something big.)

Wine-up is also one of several expressions for dancing used in *Ballad For You*.

Moreton also provides us with a fine example of a 'jamma' or work song:

(Leader)		(Chorus)
If me want for go in a Ebo	–	Me can't go there.
Since dem tief me from a Guinea	–	Me can't go there.
If me want for go in a Congo	–	Me can't go there.
Since dem tief me from my tatta	–	Me can't go there.
[father]		
If me want for go in a Kingston	–	Me can't go there.
Since massa gone in a England	–	Me can't go there.

The language of this poignant song is at least as close to modern JC as eighteenth-century peasant English is to modern working-class varieties, if not closer. We may well ask how this has come about without the stabilizing factor of literacy and print – which is said to have halted the rapid evolution of English after the advent of Caxton. Except for the word **tatta**, which is perhaps a little too 'back-a-yard', the song is in exactly the sort of language one could expect from a British Black speaker using the Creole extreme of his or her range. In fact, the song might well characterize the feeling of alienation that Blacks still feel, even though now able to go

> ina Kingston

or stay

> ina England

with the descendants of the old-time massa.

Almost in defiance of general expectations that Creole is being eradicated by schooling or rapid decreolization, broad JC does not seem to have changed much in nine generations. It seems very likely, however, that there have been some gradual changes in the phonological structure (sound system) since the early days. Cassidy writes of a feature derived from the Niger-Congo languages:

The older stages of Jamaican Creole had a feature that has almost disappeared today; the tendency to add /-i/ or /-a/ to words that would otherwise end in a consonant. [Cassidy 1961]

He then gives this example of a 'delicious caressing ... intrusive "a" ':

> Fe me own-**a** dear.

These same intruding vowels crop up in the text of 'Brixton Blues' (in Richmond 1977), a play devised by South London schoolgirls who were not aware that this feature was meant to be defunct:

> *Mum:*   ... but look what she do, do wi' me **owna** husband from America.

Plainly more could be said about the early development of the language. Very much more research remains to be done on the beginnings in West Africa and the very early stabilization of features that then developed in parallel in South America, the Caribbean and the United States.

BLACK SPEECH IN BRITAIN

Although I have stressed and will continue to stress non-English characteristics, JC is at one level a dialect of English, as we shall see. And English – that is, uncreolized English – is also the official language in Jamaica. It has been spoken by both Black and white Jamaicans since the earliest days. It is the language of books, education, the news media and much of middle-class life. All this has had its effect on the Creole – though perhaps not on its basic structure. In Britain, many Caribbean-born and virtually all British-born Black people now speak English with few or (often) no Creole features. The short story that follows, however, provides an example of the other dialect or language that Black Britons have at their disposal.

Ballad For You is an entertaining short story by Jennifer Johnson, who has lived all her life in Brixton, the heartland or 'Frontline' of Black London. The language of the story is London JC, and about three-quarters of the way along the dialect continuum towards the Creole extreme. This language may differ in subtle respects from the original Caribbean variety – and the written medium reduces the likelihood that differences in pronunciation will surface – but it is eminently recognizable as Jamaican Creole and contains examples of most of the main constructions and grammatical markers. (Chapter 4 provides a more detailed study of British Jamaican Creole, using *Ballad For You* as a reference point.)

BALLAD FOR YOU

Jennifer Johnson

Chalice and her four college friends are friendly but definitely 'high-spirited'. Trouble seems to follow them around. When they go to a party one Saturday night they soon take over; certain other girls at the party object to this but they are put firmly in their place.

dem lick head/they met up

mek a tek/let me take

soul-head/soul music fan **buck head**/met up **dem addah**/those other **a chat**/discussing

come in/seems **gal dem**/girls **a gossip**/gossiping **a**/in **a**/of

bwoy/boy

deh/is **soul-head dem**/soul fans **fi**/for

1 There is five gal I want to tell you 'bout. Dem lick head from different part a London; but is one t'ing dough, dem is one an' di same but 5 individual in every sense. Mek a tek dem one by one.

Lightening hail from Guyana an' is a soul-head. Before she buck head wid dem addah gal she couldn't 10 chat a word a bad English; now she pass CSE ina it. Why dem call she Lightening is because when dem sit down ina corner a chat people business, she always miss everyt'ing an' 15 a confuse di issue. She live up ina bush Lan', according to di addah four gal, Thornton Heath, Surrey.

Chalice come from Guyana too, but she come in jus' like a Jamaican 20 to di addah gal dem. She can chat bad an' love a gossip. She better dan any newspaper or radio. She live a North London an', out a all a dem, dis is di Top Bitch.

25 Nex' come Charlie. She is a bwoy in every sense but wid looks. She love a trouble an' always deh in di thick of it. She hate all di soul-head dem, excep' fi Lightening, because 30 she t'ink dem mad. Trouble is she

noh know seh/
doesn't know that
a goh mash up/are
going to smash up

I . . . stay?/I
wonder if all
Peckham people
are like that?
an' mash-mash/
'odd'; small
change
fi she/ her
pan/on
whey him a dhu/
what he was doing
undah manners/
showing respect
fi/for

pan/on
Front Line/
Railton Road
seh/say

seh/that

aint/don't
(general negative)
ah did seh/I said
yah soh/here
ina/in **dem**/their
Jam-Down/Jam-
aica **fi dem pick-
ney**/*their* children

noh know seh she mad too! I mean
if you a goh mash up six chair an'
set dem a fire ina de middle a di
common room dat pack up wid
35 people, somet'ing wrong some
where: I wonder is soh all Peckham
people stay?

Granny Roach is jus' four feet an'
mash-mash, but, bwoy she have di
40 biggest mout' in di world. She live a
Dulwich an' fi she family is di only
black family pan di road. She is an
only chile (thank God, him know
whey him a dhu) but, Lord, she have
45 dem whites pan she road undah
manners. An' fi a person no bigger
dan a cockroach, she have many
people walking in fear, because of
her mout'.
50 Squeakey is di last pan di list.
She live right pan di Front Line a
Brixton. So everybody kinda cagey
'bout she (so we wont seh no more
'bout she for mi noh want any con-
55 tract out pan mi life).
Now di five a dem togeddah is
not really looking fi trouble; dem is
jus' high-spirited. Soh dem seh. But
trouble love dem. Now I certain seh
60 you mus' know dis certain set a gal,
because if you noh know dem, you
aint know anybody. Like ah did seh,
two a dem come from Guyana; di
addah three born right yah soh ina
65 Inglan' but dem parents come from
Jam-Down. (Mind you, if you ask
dem parents if dem is fi dem pickney,
dem will let you know seh dem

seh/that you
woulda ... a run
it/you would have
thought *they* had
discovered Jamaica
and were
running it
yah soh/here
ina dem/in their

is man/it is men
a labrish/are
gossiping
renkest/most
cheeky, impudent
buck up/run into
anywhey/anywhere

one big queue deh/
there certainly
was (deh) a queue!
dem noh business/
they didn't care
fi full up/to fill up
naw pay/weren't
paying fi/for
dem a wait/they
were waiting
fi/to decide seh/
decided that
whey/what (do...)
in a/in fi/to
a check up/was
working out
price dem/prices
drink off/drank up

70 never seen dem before in a dem life.) But di way dem get on you woulda t'ink seh is dem discover JA an' a run it!

Back to story now. Right yah soh ina dem college there is a common
75 room known as di gossip corner, because dem gal will sit ina corner an' a laugh an' smile wid you but a chat you same time. But most of di time is man, food an' music dem a
80 labrish 'bout. Now dem is di renkest an' most bold-face set a gal you will buck up anywhey.

One morning, it was 'bout tea-break time an' dem fly upstairs to
85 di canteen. One big queue deh in front a dem but dem noh business 'bout dat. Dem jus' walk up to di front and start fi full up dem pocket wid biscuits an cheese. Dem
90 naw pay fi doze but dem will pay fi dem buns an' sandwich. Well, while dem a wait fi pay, Granny decide fi start eat she buns; but when she tek a bite she decide seh
95 she noh want it any more. Soh whey you t'ink she dhu wid it? She fling it back in a di tray an' get somet'ing else! Dem reach up fi pay now an' while di woman a check up
100 di price dem, Squeakey stan' up in front a di woman, drink off a glass

full up/filled up
fi/to **dem bold-**
face/they are bold
faced **noh di**
vicar!/the vicar!
have di mine/
wanted **whey/**
what **t'ief**/stole
a mek ... four/
making *their* eyes
and *his* eyes 'make
four' (met his
gaze directly)
start pap/began to
'pop', i.e. to come
out with

a have/was having
gal dem/girls
a plan/were
planning
whey/what a
goh/were going to
is nothin ... deh/
it was going to be
nothing but
fashion that night
(more literally:
nothing but only
(**pure**) style was
going to (be) cut
that night)
is ... gwaan/it all
happened!
did dey deh fi/
have been there to
I a goh/I am
going to

105

110

115

120

125

a orange drink, full up di glass again
an' seh she only paying fi one. Dis
is fi show you how dem bold-face.
When dem ready fi move off now,
who you t'ink a stan'-up behind
dem? Noh di vicar! An' not one a
dem a have di mine fi put back
whey dem t'ief. Dem jus' carry on
walking no an' a look ina di vicar
eye, a mek fi dem an' fi him eye
mek four. When dem reach back ina
di common room dem start pap big
laugh 'bout it.

Well, it so happened dat one a di
gal ina di college a have party pan
di satdey nite an' she invite di gal
dem. From di time dem hear 'bout
party, dem all a plan whey dem a
goh wear, because is nothing but
pure style a goh cut dah nite deh.

Well di satdey nite come an' is
one piece a t'ing gwaan. Man, you
shoulda did dey deh fi see it, but
seen as you wasn't, I a goh tell you
'bout it.

Lightening, Chalice, Charlie an'
Granny Roach arrive 'bout twelve

whey dem a dhu/
what they were
doing
Is not'ing/there's
nothing **tips**/
shoes with gold
tips
nevah seh/didn't
say
pan/at (literally
'on')
look pan/to look
at **gal dem eye**/
girls' eyes
whey/away

shame/was
ashamed
start talk/started
to talk **ina**/in

deh pan/were on

pap two move/
danced
deh/were
is dem/*they*
a control/were
controlling
**a rave strong,
strong**/were 'rav-
ing' very wildly
rub down/danced
closely
dem deh/they are
deh/there
bounce/bumped
into

130 o'clock an', as dem step in all di
man dem ina di room lef' whey dem
a dhu fi come eyes dem up an' fuss
roun' dem, like fly roun's —, because when dem gal dress, dem
sharp. Is not'ing but suit an' tips
135 wid gold dis an' gold dat.

Well di addah gal dem nevah like
it but dem nevah seh not'ing. But
one certain set start pass remark an' a
stare pan dem. Now Granny Roach
140 no like anybody look pan she. Soh
she stop dance an' look ina one a di
gal dem eye. Di gal look whey an'
Granny start dance agen. Nex' t'ing
she feel eye pan she agen; soh dis
145 time she spin roun', lif' up she skirt
an' ask di gal if she see enough yet.
Di gal shame soh till she turn she
back an' start talk. Same time in
bounce Squeakey ina she swade
150 pants suit. Man, she look hot an' all
eyes deh pan she. Di addah gal dem
all bundle roun' she fi fill her in pan
di situation. She smile an pap two
move.
155 Well now, dem all deh togeddah
an' is dem a control di middle a di
room an' a rave strong, strong. Now
Chalice is di top bitch out a all a
dem, an' she a rub down wid one a
160 di addah gal dem man. Him wont
leave her alone, but is soh she like
it, when she have addah people man
an' dem deh right deh fi see all.
Now di man woman noh like dis an'
165 she a walk pass an' a bounce Chalice.
Chalice goh fi lick her but di addah

goh fi lick/
went to hit
gal dem/girls
she fi goh fi/she
should go for

gaan/went   170
wine-up/dance
('winding'
motion)
**di man . . . fr'en
dem/**the woman   175
whose man Chalice
had been dancing
with, and her
friends
a tip-toe/were
tip-toeing
a argue/were
arguing
                             180

khu/look at
a watch/were
watching   185
box/hit   **fi/**to
a nevah/I didn't
pan/on
dem/their
                             190
deh/were   **pan/**on

is what/what
a gwaan/is going
on   **yah/**here   195
oonu/you (plural)
fi/to   **get on/**act
noh stay/isn't

gal dem stop her an' seh she fi goh
fi a walk outside.

Chalice smile 'cause she know
what dis mean. She gaan outside an'
di addah four start rave an a wine-
up ina di middle a di room. One by
one di man whey Chalice did a
dance wid woman an' she fr'en dem
a tip-toe outside. Di addah four gal
dem get on like dem noh see. Dem
give dem two minutes den charge
outside. All a dem surroun' Chalice
an' a argue.

'Alright, Granny, which one you
want?' Squeakey ask.
'Man I want dat big hefty one.'
'Khu you an' you want di biggest.'
Di addah gal dem laugh. Dem stan-
up quiet an' a watch when suddenly
Chalice box one a di gal. Dis was di
signal fi move in. Fi tell you di
truth, a nevah even see when Charlie
jump pan one a dem back an' drop-
kick di addah one. Jus' when dem
all deh pan di groun' an' a get some
box an' bruse, a voice suddenly
shout, 'Is what di raas a gwaan out
yah? Oonu young girl of today, all
oonu know is fi fight an' get on like
bad woman. Tank God my daughter
noh stay like oonu; she ina bed
where any decent young girl would
be.'

30 *Jennifer Johnson*

Dis/just

di addah gal dem/
other girls
is you dat/is that
you? **daag**/dog
a yard/at home
a noh/it wasn't
a you/to your
a road a fight/in
the road fighting

whey ... yah?/
what are you
doing out here?
is whey you deh/
where were you?

noh beat you noh/
please don't beat
you?
is what/what
whey/away

man/a man, men

fi deh a/to be in

a watch/watching

lick/blow

200 Dis gossip corner stan'-up. Dem nevah even look like dem was fighting. Di woman stan' up pan she door step ina her dressing gown a look pan dem. Di addah gal dem a 205 struggle up off di groun'.

'But wait, Lorna, is you dat,' di woman shout.

'But kiss mi daag a yard,' a noh eleven o'clock you goh a you bed 210 an' now mi see you a road a fight.'

Now, dis woman was big an' hefty an when she come wizzing pass, everybody stan' still. She grab her daughter: 'Whey you a dhu out 215 yah? Is whey you deh?'

'I was at the party, mommy, oh please don't beat me.'

'Noh beat you noh. Is what you was fighting ovah gal?'

220 'Dem trying to teck whey my boyfriend.'

'You what? Man? You have man? Gal, you can't even wash you draws good an' a fight over man when 225 you suppose fi deh a you bed. You have man. Well I going show you 'bout man you see, love.'

Well, by now all di people from di party outside a watch while dis 230 woman teck off her slipper an' plant a lick ina dis gal head. Man, I nevah see a woman beat her daughter soh

fawdah/father

fr'en' dem/friends
a pap/were
'popping'
fi ... up/to come
and try to ruin

a/I

a goh/are going
a party/to a party
fi dey-deh/to be
there

in all my life. An' when di fawdah
come out it was like murder. When
235 dem done, dem jus' drag her inside.
Her fr'en' dem disappear long time
an' di gossip corner gal dem a pap
some big laugh.

'Dat will teach dat gal fi come
240 try mash up my scene,' Chalice seh,
an' di addahs agree.

Like a did seh, is one piece a
t'ing gwaan: an' seeing it is bettah
dan reading it. Soh anytime you a
245 goh a party, mek sure you suppose
fi dey-deh. If not, watch you step
'cause di gossip corner might be
there. An' dem don't want you man,
jus' a bit a fun. An' it may be at
250 your expense.

CHAPTER 2

Language, Culture and Identity

Black cultures of the New World have had a considerable impact on modern Western culture, and the influence is growing. It could be argued that in certain areas, such as music and language, Blacks are a major source of vitality and innovation, yet paradoxically Black people of the West Indies and North America are frequently regarded as having little or no separate culture of their own. Even some West Indians talk of their lack of culture, identity, separate language, and so on. The reasons for all this are most complex, but they derive from the experience of slavery. Before slavery there were the ancestral identities: Ibo, Yoruba, Ashanti, Efik, Ewe, Mandinka, Wolof, and so on. Sometime between Queen Anne and Queen Victoria most of the African words and the African ethnic identities that went with them were erased from the West Indian consciousness:

... it was the whites who took our culture away from us in the first place. I an I thought Jah gave each an every race their own language so no other than that race can overstan [understand] them but it is through we were taken from our forefathers' land and taken into slavery and now in a Babylon that we speak the white tongue ... [Sis Zulekia Moore, letter in *Voice of Rasta*, no. 18]

This is the expression of a common view, couched here in Rastafarian imagery. In a sense Black people also lost their history, and, as Mohammed Ali once said, without history they were 'walking dead men'. History is a kind of identity carried on through time.

Some of the lost history is, of course, recoverable, and although the words were lost the languages were not. The individual African tongues disappeared but the Creoles that replaced them remained essentially non-European languages carrying more than 90 per cent European vocabulary – English words in the case of Jamaican for instance, and French in the case of Haitian. Even the words derived from European languages have become as Creole as the other components of the languages. If we look at the relationship between English and contributing European languages we can see a parallel case where the words **candle** and **prayer**, for example, are no longer French words. English in fact has remained a Germanic language, though now carrying a vocabulary that is largely *non*-Germanic in origin.

Language provides a parable for what has happened to Caribbean cultures as a whole. Firstly, in language and in culture generally there has been a blending of various influences, but the strongest influence, at least at grass roots level, is African. Moving from grass roots to the middle class the African element tends to be removed or at least buried deeper – although West Indian readers will consider this a great simplification.

Secondly, both language and, to a lesser extent, other areas of culture are organized at various different levels. In language, for example, when young human beings learn to talk they start with the intonation level that they begin practising when only a few months old. At the same time they begin to utter or try to utter the vowel sounds and consonants. After that they embark on the indefinitely long process of learning the vocabulary of the language. Then the higher levels of organization are gradually learned in order to produce coherent meaningful speech: the morphology (grammatical markers or inflections), the syntax (grammatical constructions) and the discourse level (the organization of sentences and parts of sentences into coherent 'paragraphs' of speech or coherent dialogues with others). Finally, but perhaps at a surprisingly early age, speakers begin to learn special styles of speaking to achieve socially recognized ends: entertainment, manipulation, control, self-advertisement, and so on. If we look at how the dialect continuum between Jamaican Creole and standard English works on the different levels we can see that, in shifting between the two, first the morphology begins to alter, then pronunciation, while the syntax and the intonation are more resistant to change. As we have seen, the vocabulary level of a language is the most volatile of all, and literally thousands of words from outside sources can be incorporated into a language without altering it fundamentally. Looking at culture as a whole we can see some areas that stubbornly resist change, and others where new input is freely received. However, this new input is often retextured to fit with the general grain of the culture.

Finally, to complete the analogy, there is the Caribbean cultural habit of 'syncretism' and 'remodelling'. In these processes African and European elements (words, constructions, gestures, etc.) become bonded together. One linguistic example would be Creole **se**, derived from Twi/Ibo **se** (meaning either 'quote follows' or 'that' used as a complementizer) but becoming identified with English **say**. Remodelling is the term used especially to describe the masking or camouflaging of Creole items when using English or talking/behaving in an 'English' context. These amount to cultural puns. An example might occur when a Creole speaker 'thinks' **I feel say** but says **I feel to say that**, which is nearer standard English in form. The well-known song 'Brown Girl in the Ring' provides an altogether more subtle example of remodelling: 'She look(s) like a sugar in a plum'. This is English (of a nonsensical kind). However, the pronunciation has only to be tuned slightly toward Creole – 'Shi look lakah sugar iina plum' – and **like** becomes the broad Jamaican Creole **lakah** and **in** becomes **iina** swallowing up the indefinite article, which is now not needed before 'plum', as this has become a Creole generic noun meaning 'plums in general' or 'any plum'.

All these considerations – different levels of organization, continua, blending of elements and resistance – can be seen *to some extent* in other aspects of the culture: gesture, social behaviour (including family life and associated attitudes), music, dancing and worship. For the remainder of the chapter, however, I shall concentrate on the oral culture, and come finally to a brief appreciation of West Indian ways, expressed through language, of holding an identity together under stress.

BRITISH BLACK VERBAL ART

In the studies of linguists such as Labov and Mitchell-Kernan working on Black American vernacular, focus of interest has tended to be on skilful creative impromptu uses of language: verbal duelling, rifting, fancy talk, signifying, rapping, loud-talking, marking. Before looking at this more dynamic side of the equivalent British Black culture, however, let us look at what we might call the folkloristic side – oral literature proper. There is, however, no sharp division between these two sides. Expressions of folklore are very often 'dynamic' (in a sense that still has to be defined) and dynamic, im-promptu uses of language frequently draw on traditional material.

Folklore/oral literature

This is an area of culture where we find not only elements that have been handed down for centuries – Anansi stories for instance – but also recently incorporated elements that may be shown to have circulated far and wide. The Opies (1977) have remarked on this fact in connection with British children's playground culture; some parts of the traditional culture are very localized and resistant to outside influences, and other items (often ephemera) diffuse widely over very large areas, perhaps right across the world. In this context it is not constructive for teachers to be disappointed when the first folk tale their Black pupils tell them is, say, 'The Three Pigs'. Of course, as I have already observed, these free-flowing elements will not enter a culture unless they fit.

Folk tales
Black children in Britain have inherited a living tradition of orally transmitted folk tales. At the core of the tradition are the tales of Anansi spider, and other typically Caribbean tales common to the Black culture of widely separated islands and territories. Of the non-African stories that have added to the tradition, the Asian stories are probably the most important – especially in Trinidad and Guyana. Immogen, an Afro-Trini-dadian girl, said: 'Those of my Indian friends [in Trinidad]

told me a lot of stories.' One of the tales that she herself narrated was a version of 'The Wolf and the Kids' in which the three kids were called Minibo, Minibatani and Kakarajit. Dorita, also Afro-Trinidadian, told me many stories, and several of these seemed different from what we might call typical Caribbean material. They were considerably longer than most Anansi stories and conjured up a world of palaces, kings, princesses, courtyards and gardens – in contrast to the usual sparely-described, timeless, placeless world of the spider man and his animal dupes. By pure serendipity I happened to ask an Indian-born Punjabi girl, Bimla, to tell a folk story at about this time. Her tale was basically the same as one of Dorita's. It was the story of a king and his seven wives, whose youngest wife, despised by the rest, eats a soiled mango and then gives birth to a monkey. So though both girls had come to Bedford from countries on opposite sides of the world they had heard the 'same' story back home.

   Dorita was fond of the supernatural and recounted tales of 'lija bless or diablesse – lovely ladies with 'one cow foot and one human foot' concealed beneath their gowns, who accost young men on the road and try to bewitch them. Dorita said that her own cousin had had a narrow escape from one such deadly female. Here, however, is her tale of the sukunyah (or soucouyen), the skin-changing vampire:

Once my cousin, his friend was a sukunyah. She used to deal [i.e. in magic]. So one day everybody tellin' him that how your friend deals and he didn't believe them – because his friend wouldn't do him nothing but she will suck other people and take away their blood inside them. And one day this woman, she was ever so wicked to people that deal, so she was ever so angry because the sukunyah suckin' every baby that she have, and killin' all her animals. So one day she *grind* pepper and she *mash* up pepper and salt with her timble ... timber. She mash them up and everybody help her with ... everybody have things with ... Everybody start punging [pounding] with a martel, mortar 'tick. Everybody pung it. And all the sukunyah, when she *take* out her skin, and she *went* out, they take the pepper and they spread it right over her skin. And as she go to put her skin burn she and she bawl: 'skin, skin, don't hurt me, don't hurt me skin, skin, skin!'

Except where Dorita is casting around for the old vocabulary of 'martels' and mortar sticks, her delivery is flowing and rhythmic. The blood sucking witch (whose vulnerability is that she leaves her skin at home when she goes about her business) roams abroad not only in Trinidad but the other French Creole speaking islands of the Caribbean. In Jamaica she is called the Old Hige (Hag) and calls out in consternation 'Kin you no know me?' She has even been reported in the Black American South (cf. Jackson 1967).

Of course, Anansi himself has a special place in Black cultures over a vast area. As most readers will know, Anansi came from West Africa where he is still flourishing. His exploits are celebrated in many West African tales. In Ashanti lore, Krokroko the great spider symbolizes wisdom; he is a trickster god comparable to an extent with Legba of the Dahomeyans. The Hare/Brer Rabbit and Anansi together unite West Africa with nearly the whole of the vernacular Black cultures of the New World, including Black cultures in Latin America. These two tricksters crossed the Atlantic with the Africans as a part of what can now be seen as an immense spiritual cargo. The Hare and the Spider are not just African survivals, they *are* African survival. They symbolize the will to survive and thrive under adverse conditions, through always being ready to work their plan on the characters around them. When Anansi speaks he 'doubles the tongue as the Africans do' (quote from a tape of a Jamaican man recorded by Ruth Hibbert in London). And yet he is supremely at home in his surroundings. The very fact that Anansi can change back into a spider and scuttle up into the rafters to escape suggests adaptability – at a price. Ironically the spiderman is not a hero in the classic sense; perhaps anti-hero would be a more apt description. In several of the tales recorded in Bedford his plans go awry even when he has good intentions, as in this crisp version written down, with the notes, by Mrs M. A. Carter (Jamaican):

Anansi Baths his Mother

One day Brer Nancy's mother was sick and needed a bath, but Annancy was the only child. He decided to give her a bath; so he told all his friends that he was going to do so. He went and collected bush [herbs] to boil the bath.

When the bath was ready he poured it into the pan. He put her in the pan of bath which was too hot – and her teeth skinned [skin-teeth = to bare the teeth without smiling]. Not knowing that this bath was too hot, he took her out, put her back to bed and went and told all his friends that his mother was so pleased with her bath because she had not stopped laughing since.

He was quite pleased with himself until he realized she was dead.

Though this is a particularly succinct tale, very many tellings of Anansi stories are marked by this economy of expression, with a swift-moving plot and little side-tracking on description – in this they are not unlike jokes. However, Anansi stories are quite often composite, which can make them considerably longer. One well-known story or 'motif' will link itself to another and produce such a tale as the one told by April (see Texts). April was born in Britain and was only 8 years old when she told with some apparent improvisation her composite tale of Brother Haansi (Anansi) and Brother Brown, which she had learned from her uncle.

Through all the numberless tales and variants of tales in which Anansi figures there is a common thread of disreputable, indomitable humanity that is instantly recognizable. This thread runs back to West Africa and the days before the Middle Passage. As such, it is in itself a collective identity projected through time, so perhaps to some extent it makes up for the lost history. In urban Britain some say that Anansi is no longer 'relevant'. Possibly other myths will have to take over – it is difficult to judge at this time. But plainly we should not underestimate Anansi.

Proverbs

Proverbs have an important place in many cultures. They are part of the communal wisdom of ordinary people. It is quite possible that English people underrate this type of folklore, which acts as a mirror for society and the individual, as novelist John Berger has pointed out. Proverbs are cherished in the Caribbean: they season and illustrate everyday conversation, they are used as a tool of instruction, or as a weapon of verbal defence (cf. Barrett 1976: 39).

Whoever would understand Jamaican and other Caribbean cultures from which the Black cultural background in Britain has evolved would do well to look at these proverbs. They go to the heart of the matter as a knife goes to the heart of a yam. Afro-Caribbean and African ideals of deference and obedience are expressed in the Trinidad/Tobagan:

> Pickney weh [who] nuh hear wha e mumma say
> does have to drink hot water without sugar.

Compare the Tshiluba of Zaire who say:

> Muana Kutuma, muana Kudia; muana tshishiku,
> muana nzalu. (The obedient child gets to eat;
> the disobedient one goes hungry.)

African-derived Caribbean reticence is expressed in:

> Talk half lef half.

or

> Mouth open, story jump out.

Ideals of decorum are succinctly conveyed in:

> Howdye come from door.

(social convention demands that a visitor give the first greeting) and

> Howdye and tanky, bruk no square.

i.e. politeness hurts no one. In West Indian societies it is thought particularly impolite not to greet an acquaintance or any person one passes on the road. To take an example from a well-known folk story, Brer Rabbit behaves like a good Afro-American in becoming incensed at the Tar baby's refusal to return his greeting.

The ideal of non-confrontation is expressed in the Trinidad/Tobagan:

> Hat tum better than beg pardon.
> (Better not to say a thing than have to apologise
> for having said it.)

Some readers may find this a particularly unlikely Caribbean ideal. But Caribbean life is full of paradoxes. The generally upheld norms of non-confrontation are expected to be broken occasionally when one just has to undam one's feelings. There also seem to be inter-island differences here whereby Jamaicans see themselves as more volatile than the rest; Anguillans seem by comparison almost oriental in their accommodation although, as they say themselves, when finally they are aroused, 'watch out'. Many younger generation Black people in Britain also tend to view this norm as obsequious, particularly where it is used towards whites in authority. However, 'indirection', reticence and non-confrontation are still commonly met with.

Several commentators have characterized Caribbean and other Creoles as devoid of abstract vocabulary and so (it is at least implied) incapable of expressing abstract thought:

As with the other French Creoles, the Seychelles Creole is ornate and colourful, but it has some shortcomings. It has no orthography, being only spoken, and it cannot be used to express abstractions. Because of these shortcomings creole does not deserve the status of a distinct language. [Lionnet 1972: 111]

No one who is acquainted with Caribbean proverbs could, logically, persist in this sort of view, unless he also thought that John Donne was not ultimately expressing abstract ideas in his poetry and prose when he chose to use concrete images in the form of metaphor and simile. In their different ways both Caribbean proverbs and Donne's writing are peculiarly vivid because they draw striking comparisons between hitherto unconnected things in order to put across an idea. It is mistaken, incidentally, to think that Creoles lack abstract nouns *per se*. Very often, particularly in the proverbs, other parts of speech (adjectives or whole clauses) are appropriated to play the part of abstract nouns, as in:

Hungry hungry and **full full** no travel same pass.
(Hunger and plenty do not travel the same road.)

The effect of proverbial technique can be that of compression:

Sabby-so mek mekso ' tan' so.

Cundall (1972) renders this into English as 'upon the understanding of a thing depends how it is accomplished'. Like Biblical parables, proverbs are often cryptic. Sometimes this is because they are too sparely expressed to be readily understood – almost like riddles. The Anguillans have a proverb:

Experience is a bull.

This needs to be explicated. It is a bull in that at first, perhaps, experience renders no benefit to its owner. In the fullness of time, however, it can offer service that is very highly prized not only by its owner but by his neighbours.

Other proverbs are cryptic because they are compressed fables or references to fables. Michael Rosen gives an example:

I overheard Monica in the first year [of Vauxhall Manor School] say, 'Poor George and his Jackass.' 'What's that mean?' I said. 'It's a bit like – he bit off more than he could chew – he got more than he bargained for' she said. 'Who was George?' I asked. She told me – but I didn't have a tape recorder handy, so I asked her to write it down for me. Her mother comes from Jamaica:

Sometimes my mum, she doesn't usually tell stories but say old proverbs like this one called Poor George and his Jackass. One day George was returning by night on his Jackass when all of a sudden a duppy [ghost] stopped him and got on the jackass with him and rode all the way home with him. That night the jackass died of shock, and George was sick for a while, and that is the way we get the saying of Poor George and his Jackass.

(Spelling corrected for 'doesn't' and 'usually'.) [M. Rosen n.d.]

Like poetry, proverbs are (sometimes) open to different interpretation – depending on the locality in which they are used (in Jamaica) and the context in which they are used. We also find that virtually the same proverb occurs in widely separated areas of the Caribbean or in Africa. Take the expression:

Cockroach never get justice when chicken judges.

That is, an underdog cannot expect justice. In Trinidad this occurs in both French and English Creole versions:

Cockroach nuh have right in fowl party.
Ravette pas jamais tener raison devant poule.

Virtually the same French Creole version occurs in Haiti and Louisiana. African languages have:

In a court of fowls the cockroach never wins his
    case. (Kikongo)

and

Maize has no rights with the hen. (Yoruba)

Proverbs have become just as amazingly diffused across the
globe as folk stories – selectively diffused, of course, for as
Jamaicans say 'deaf ears give story carrier trouble'. However,
a primary source of both the tradition and the individual
proverbs of the Caribbean seems to be Africa. More systematic, detailed scrutiny of sources is necessary before one can
be positive about this. What we are able to say at this point
is that, where parallel examples can be found outside the
Caribbean and Black America, the clear majority are either
solely African, or African *and* European. Many that are not
found in Europe occur in very similar form in far-flung areas
of the Afro-American world and in many West African
cultures (and to a lesser extent in Central Africa and other
areas of the Sub-Saharan continent). A large body of the
'purely African' proverbs involve animals in talking and
acting like human beings, conjuring up the concrete but
mythical world of Brer Anansi, Brer Rabbit, and the tortoise
and the hare. The ten proverbs below illustrate this cultural
continuity from the Old World (primarily Africa) to the New:

(1) Jamaican:

Rain nebber fall a one man door.
[cf. The rain falleth on the just and the unjust.
    Matthew 5 v. 45][1]

Black American:

It rains and everyman feels it someday.

Yoruba (Nigeria):

The rain does not recognize anyone as friend.
Whomsoever it sees it drenches.

This occurs also in Nyang (Cameroon).

[1] Readers may be interested in a version of this collected from my
father-in-law: 'The rain falleth on the just and unjust fellow, but
chiefly on the just, because the unjust has the just's umbrellow'.

(2) Jamaican:

> Seven year no 'nough fe wash freckle off a guinea hen back.

Black American:

> Seven years is not too long for a rabbit to wear a rough bosom shirt.

Ashanti (Ghana):

> When rain beats on a leopard it wets him but it does not wash out his spots.

(3) Jamaican:

> When fowl drink water him say 'tank God'. When man drink water him say nuttin'.
> [Fowls are said to lift their heads after drinking.]

Ashanti (Ghana):

> When a fowl drinks water it (first) takes it and shows it to the Supreme Being.

(4) Jamaican:

> When breeze no blow you no see fowl back.
> (Character is brought out by trying circumstances.)

Haitian:

> Ce l'he'r vent ca venter, moune ca we'r lapeau poule.

Hausa (Nigeria, Chad, Volta):

> The wind has blown, we have seen the chicken's rump.

This occurs in Trinidadian and in other African languages – for instance in Kinyarwanda (Rwanda).

(5) Jamaican:

> You nebber see empty bag 'tan' up.
> (If you are hungry you cannot work.)

Haitian:

> Sac qui vide pas connait rete debout.

Mende (Mali, Guinea):

An empty sack will not stand up by itself.

This proverb, which also occurs in Martinique, has European parallels (in English, Italian, German, Estonian and so on) and is quoted in George Eliot's *Mill on the Floss*.

(6) Trinidadian:

What hut [hurts] eye does mek nose run.

Yoruba (Nigeria):

The disease which affects the eye usually affects the nose as well.

This occurs in other African languages including Duala, Nyang and Ibo.

(7) Jamaican:

Talk is the ears' food.

Trinidadian:

Causer ce manger zoreies.

Ibo (Nigeria):

Tales are the food of the ear.

(8) Jamaican:

Cashew nebber bear guava.

Trinidadian:

Guinea hen carn bring ram goat.

Haitian:

Giramou pas donne calabasse.

Oji (Ghana):

The daughter of a crab does not give birth to a bird.

(9) Jamaican:

Wha' you know a day, you can' take fire-'tick fe look for a night.

Ewe (Togo, Ghana):

> That which one sees in the day time one need not
> seek with torches.

This also occurs in Trinidadian.

(10) Jamaican:

> You can't eat ochra soup with one finger.

Ewe (Togo, Ghana):

> One finger alone cannot drink the soup.

The same or similar versions of this proverb occur in Trinidadian and African languages – Basa (Liberia and Nigeria), Jukun and Nyang.

Before we leave the subject it is important to register that this is still a living tradition feeding into various verbal art forms, including verbal duelling where one can use proverbs to denigrate one's opponent (as will be made more apparent later in this chapter). Something of the style of proverbs persists in conversation even if proverbs themselves are not used, as in this quotation from a Rastaman in discursive style, where he describes the alienation that he feels from British society:

It is inevitable that we, as black people, were never and can never be part of this country where we do not belong; like a heart transplant it rejects us. [Cashmore 1979: 83]

Proverbs and the ideas that they embody also feed into reggae lyrics. The widely known 'Lilly [little] axe can cut down big tree' surfaces in a recent hit by Bob Marley:

> If you are a big tree
> We are a small axe
> Sharpened to cut you down.

Certain Caribbean poets have also drawn on the proverbial style. Edward Brathwaite's 'The Dust' is a most notable example, peculiarly successful in penetrating to the timelessness beyond the everyday, as the best proverbs are able to do. Even more obviously Louise Bennett, the Jamaican poet, directly borrows the style of the Jamaican proverb in 'Dutty tuff' (The ground is hard):

> Sun a-shine but tings noh bright,
> Doah Pot a-bwile, bickle noh noff,
> River flood but water scarce yaw
> Rain a-fall but Dutty tuff!

> **Doah**/though   **a-bwile**/is boiling   **bickle noh noff**/there's not much food   **yaw**/indeed

There is a triangular relationship here. Proverbs and their style are feeding into both reggae and poetry. At the same time the dividing line between poetry and reggae is blurred, since Jamaican poetry is primarily written to be spoken aloud, or even declaimed or 'dubbed' over music. Reggae, incidentally, is performing the function that proverbs traditionally have always done: holding a mirror up to the culture, and also providing guidance.

Riddles and rhyming games

Riddles are a popular part of vernacular culture in the Caribbean. As Martha Beckwith points out, there is a connection between riddles and the pithy and often metaphorical Caribbean proverbs: 'The art [of a proverb] differs therefore from that employed in the folk riddle only by expressing in the terms of the comparison an observation upon life rather than a mere object of everyday experience' (Beckwith 1929: 201). In other words, riddles are purely for fun (although they are a kind of 'play' with imagery that develops elasticity of mind) and unlike proverbs they are very much a feature of peer group language play. Children, and sometimes adults too, enjoy riddles in many cultures. Caribbean riddles are different from the ones British children have traditionally asked in that they are frequently posed in the form of a statement, not a question, and usually are cryptic rather than purely punning – like those in the riddling match between Bilbo and Gollum in *The Hobbit*. Here are some examples from early twentieth-century Jamaica and late twentieth-century Black Britain:

Jamaica:

Riddle me riddle, guess me this riddle, and perhaps not:

John Redman tickle John Blackman till he laugh, pooka-pooka.

Answer: a kettle on a fire.

Going up to town all cry, coming home all are silent.

Answer: feet. [In the damp of the morning bare feet make a sound; coming home in the afternoon footfalls are silent.]

Dere was a lady – five constabs went fe him, two bring him, two pass sentence an execute him.

Answer: a flea and the five fingers.

Bedford/Jamaican:

Pickney ina bus. All a dem head red.

Answer: matches in a match box.

My father have a horse, he ride it till his back was sore.

Answer: a roof top.

There was a man, he have buttons from his head to he foot.

Answer: a pineapple.

All England dead and never rotten.

Answer: a bottle [because it never rots].

Sweet water standing.

Answer: sugar cane.

Bedford/Trinidadian:

O-riddle-a-riddle-ee-dee. Something stands up, Something fall down. What is it?

Answer: cane (sugar cane).

O-riddle-a-riddle-ee-dee. I saw an old man weh he wee so fast, he make me laugh. Riddle-ee-dee. What was that?

Answer: a tap.

'My Father has' is a common opening formula for riddles and is said to refer to the 'Supreme Being'.

Together with dipping and skipping rhymes and other playground poems and chants, riddles provide a steady flow of poetic activity for children, even those said to live in 'poemless slums' Here I must stress both the similarities and the differences between Caribbean and English play culture particularly at primary school age. As we have seen, Caribbean riddles are distinctive, but white children enjoy riddles too, including the cryptic type:

> What goes under the water, on the water and over
>   the water and never gets wet?
> *Answer:* an egg in a duck's belly.

A number of the rhymes and the games in both cultures are similar, but the approach of the Black children to this common material is frequently different – a matter of style. For example, the rhyme:

> Glory glory halleluiah,
> Teacher hit me with a ruler,
> The ruler broke in half,
> And the class began to laugh,
> On the last day of September.

is known in Bedford, and the Opies recorded it in Lincolnshire. A variant of it was noted by Labov as a New York children's rhyme. It occurs in Jamaica too, but the Jamaican version I have heard was sung with a rhythmic beat and the singer kept returning to the first two lines, so the verse structure shown above was altered. Dorothea Thompson noted that when Black children and white played together there were instances where white children found the Black style attractive and adopted it themselves. She mentions ring games such as the ubiquitous 'Brown Girl in the Ring' (Caribbean) and 'Jenny is a-weeping' (played by white English children);

The coloured children use a pelvic gyration which Elder mentions as 'winding' and is very closely bound up with the Jamaican culture. This movement has been adopted by our children extensively in their games. [Thompson 1975: 12]

Thompson adds:

The coloured children excel in and have taught our children their idea of rhythmic clapping to a song – 'who stole the cookie from the cookie jar'. [p.12]

Notice, incidentally, that this quoted line is in standard English. As I have mentioned above, these rhymes can usually be said with a wide range of dialect nuance involving only minimal alteration to the wording.

The Caribbean voice

The oral culture we have been looking at is obviously worth study and appreciation. However, Afro-American language culture is especially distinctive in its creative use of language in apparently impromptu situations. I am not thinking so much of manipulative language here, though that has an important place, as of language that is used to entertain and impress. It becomes apparent that young Black people in the Caribbean (and in Britain) and in the United States, frequently seek to improve confident fluent use of language, particularly in the peer group, and that verbal styles for specific purposes are developed: taunting, cursing, narrating, toasting, boasting and so on. These frequently become performances in the manner mentioned earlier. This means that feedback from the 'audience' is expected. The personality of the speaker may be felt to come through strongly, but it also takes on a ritual quality because to varying degrees the speaker is assuming a role – almost a theatrical role. Moreover, the voice is used consciously in a way that might be described as 'dynamic' (the dictionary definition of dynamic is 'imparting force'). All dominantly oral culture is dynamic in that sound is an event rather than an object, and cannot be static.

What is distinctively dynamic about Black oral language? Simply that the use of the voice itself seems to celebrate this dynamic quality – to project it. This is a quality that pervades the culture and that is difficult to describe because the terminology is lacking – or at least white Americans and Europeans lack it. Abrahams suggests that 'it would be easy to get at the Afro-American aesthetic by objective descriptions of ways of handling metric impulses (through multi-meter or polyrhythm) or relationship of voices or movements (through a high incidence of overlap and interlock between the participants in the performance) ... ' (Abrahams 1976: 81). Abrahams concludes that such an approach would not be true to the material. It would certainly be simpler at any rate to say that in Black speech events the voice is consciously used to generate (varying degrees of) excitement – or force in the case of tough use of language for control. Of course this is a generalization about a culture, not individuals. Let us begin by looking at what might be called 'ordinary' narrative, where the performance element is relatively subdued. In fact, any narrative whether from a Black or white person takes on a variable amount of 'performance' quality ranging from that of a colourless account (such as a write-up of a scientific experiment) to that of a dramatic monologue. In the Bedford research (Sutcliffe 1978) a Jamaican boy entertained me with a large number of descriptive narratives on Jamaican country life. Unlike the stereotype I have been putting forward, this boy, Martin, had a quiet 'thin' voice, a compressed tonal range, and at times a slightly jerky, *un*rhythmic delivery. Nonetheless his narratives were superb. His strength lay, in the first place, in his involvement with his subject and his sensitive grasp of detail. On guinea pigs:

The rough-raw guinea pig, we call that one Rough Raw because it different, it all shaggy-up. But the hair don't lay down like the other one – we call the other one Smooth, Smooth, guinea pig.

On the abundance in the countryside:

There was mango tree with different common mango, beef mango, all kind a mango. Long mango. And we pick and eat and carry home again. And cashew, cashew. We play marble with cashew you know? ... And sometime we roast them, and eat them like peanut, common nut, and put salt on them ... I saw a lot of big red mango. We call the mango-dem bobi mango because they used to have titty, titty on them.

On setting snares (chokie) for birds:

But they scared you know. Everytime they push their head they take it out and look, and put it in and take it out and look, till the last time now they put it in, keep it in there, and then you go so – wam! If it [the string] draw too hard it will break and they will drop out. You just have to take your time and draw it down.

Here he describes the birds' movements exactly as if they were happening before him, rather than generalizing: 'they kept putting their heads in and out of the snare'. In the same way he always seems to use direct rather than indirect speech. He attributes speech to himself to comment on the action – in Labov's terminology this means that the evaluation (comment) is *embedded* or woven into the speech/action:

So mi go down deh [the river] and mi look. And mi push mi hand underneat' wash-stone ... an mi feel a big janga, tamba [types of crayfish]. It bite mi. Mi seh 'yuh bite mi but mi nah let yuh go, mi nah let yuh go!'

In what is possibly the best narrative of all, the catching of the big 'Aunty Katie' (the Golden Oriole), he again expresses his feelings through his own direct speech:

> The bird fly away
> and gone.
> I was very cross.
> And I start to swear to meself
> 'Oh, that bird get away
> and me could have it to eat.'

His cry of delight when he finally catches the Aunty Katie is a re-enactment of what actually happened but also, in its rhythm and repetition, brings the story to a dramatic conclusion:

> He-e-ey! I catch a bird!
> I catch a bird!
> I catch a Aunty Katie, Aunty Katie, Aunty Katie!

Here, and elsewhere, while telling an 'ordinary' narrative, Martin used a device to mark climax that occurs too often and is too much akin to devices in the folk tales of (say) Dorita to be accidental. Compare Dorita's ending to the sukunyah story, and compare the cry of the thwarted 'lija bless – the one who tried to 'get' Dorita's cousin:

> Ke, ke, ke, kyu lai!
> You lucky I didn't get you tonight!
> I get you another day!

Mention was made earlier of the blurred distinction between folklore, oral literature and the 'improvised' speech styles we are now considering. There is an unbroken range from Martin's narratives, through mythical (?) happenings described as real – e.g. Dorita's 'true' story of her cousin and the 'lija bless – to old stories set in the real world, such as Dorita's telling of the sukunyah, and finally to other folk tales that have no claim to reality. And this is just one example of the blurred distinction.

Martin's narratives, deceptively underplayed though they are, tend to take on the performance styles of the more ritual use of language that I shall look at briefly below. This becomes apparent too when one notices how few hesitations and false starts there are – because he is using techniques of parallel phrasing and repetition that can be seen to be an intrinsic part of much Black dramatic oral language. However, his main aim seems to be to handle what he has to say competently, rather than to dramatize himself or his subject in too obvious a manner. He has so much to say about his sorely missed life around the river, the bush, the coffee piece and the gungo walk.

Frequently, though, the aim of the young British Black narrator is to dramatize and entertain in a way that produces feedback from the audience. One can see informal groups of people in a half circle around a speaker who is using techniques such as mimicry or playing with different shades of dialect to gossip – or labrish – or to narrate a story as involved as *Ballad For You*. (*BFY* in fact is a written performance of such a style, although of course the reader has to create the performance quality anew.) Sometimes, in an effort really to 'cut style' or put oneself or one's group forward by boasting, Black British narratives take on an even more noticeable ritual quality. This shows in the rhythmic delivery, the voice, the use of formulaic phrasing, and also in a marked use of the parallel phrasing, repetition and emphasis I have already mentioned. Angela's narrative, which also appears in V. K. Edwards (1979b: 53) is a good example. It is particularly interesting because the speaker (then aged 14) is from a middle-class home and has had to 'stretch' herself to acquire the speaking styles of the group she aspires to belong to.

I leave it to readers to analyse its structure. The structure of repetitions and the formulae 'mek/let mi tell you' and so on (in *Ballad For You* it is 'mek a tek', etc.) are there not only to underline verbally; they allow the narrator respite to think ahead. Such techniques are found in the sermons of Black preachers, and indeed in other oral cultures. (Compare, for example, the techniques in 'Beowulf' or the 'Battle of Maldon'.) More than that they enable her to preserve the rhythm, which is strong in this recording. In this rhythmic style Angela has moved far from local English narrative style – which at all events operates in a linguistic system, or more particularly a stress and intonation system, that is completely different:

> Well two week ago yuh know
> wi's jus' comin' from school you see.
> You wa:n see fifty people a-go down London Road, sa!
> An' let mi tell yuh one time
> wi's walkin' down half way down London Road, yuh know.
> An see Sheila and Enid
> and everybody a-walk pas' dem sa!
> An everybody a-jumble roun' dem.
> When they reach half way down London Road, you know,
> down near dat place down deh.
> Le' mi tell you one time,
> they start a-fight yuh see,
> One piece of fight!
> Dey started to roll pan agrong [on the ground] you know,
> *Roll!* Let mi tell yuh when they roll they really roll.
> Den 'ey get up an' start glarin' at each oda.
> Bout fifti people was roun' deh,
> an deh woz people stan'in outside dem door a-watch.
> So mi walk home.
> When mi come to school on Monday morning,
> come from a place an' deh a-walk.
> When mi fin' wha' di teacher come h'ax mi
> fi come stan' up dere wid di headmaster deh,
> him sen' all of us, all of us, down into him h'office
>   and him tek out him cane.
> If dat man did eva cane me, him woulda fin' out
>   somep'n today!

In addition to the dramatic performance aspect there is an associated tendency for ordinary conversation to become a competitive 'happening'. One speaker will subtly or overtly seek to outdo another both by what he says and the way he says it. This debate element has been connected with the conflicting value systems of the Caribbean background: peergroup versus home, reputation versus respectability, and African versus European. The essence is to play with these ideas without too much real involvement and 'take the shame and don't complain' if one is outdone. While this approach to life can cause real contention – Labov has focused on the importance for the speakers of being able to distinguish between ritual and real insult (1972: 341) – it also engenders group feeling and provides endless entertainment. The results can be entertaining even when read from a transcript of a tape, which of course is a poor substitute for the oral performance. There is a range of different styles, from 'ordinary' dialogue with subtly competitive elements through to highly ritualized verbal duelling. There is also the distinction between a dialogue and a group performance in which everyone seems to be talking at once (in contra-distinction to the most common European pattern of turn-taking in conversation with efforts made to avoid voice overlap). The subject is too demanding and complex for anything like a full analysis to be presented at this point. Instead I shall limit the account to two main examples, the first being an example of competitive speech operated as dialogue, and the second of group performance.

Gregory and Peter were 10-year-olds at the time of recording in 1974. Peter is British born of non-Jamaican Caribbean parents. Gregory – whose use of distinctive 'Black voice' is striking – comes from a Black American family. They had already established a reputation, amongst staff and other children of the school that they attended, for having a good line in repartee – in fact they introduced an Italian boy as their agent! Both Black children seek to 'put the other down' by telling a pejorative tale of the other's poor circumstances or stupidity. (Similar techniques are known as 'signifying' in Black American culture.)

Gregory: Hey, Peter. Look, I heard something about, you know, when you was 2 years old. I heard that, when you was small, that if you put a piece of cheese on the floor, near to your big toe, a rat would come and eat the piece of cheese and your big toe with it. You know that?

Peter: ùh-ùh.

Gregory: I heard that from your mother.
I heard that, when you was sitting on your bed, one day when your mum came inside the room with your bottle, you were so overjoyed that you fell off the bed.

Peter: One day, um, I heard from my sister, when she was riding down Clarendon Street that you ... er ... you ... walking along the road when you were 2 years old and you had very, very bony legs. And with all your bony legs there was this dog come along and he chases for all your bony legs. I remember that.

Gregory: Now you listen to me, mate. I don't find that funny. What about when you came out this taxi when you was about 7 years old? Yeah, you're sorta rich, and you drop about all your coppers on the floor. And now, there was this boxer dog, following all your coppers along the floor, and he come and see you, with a hole in your trousers, and he get hold of your thing and bite it off.

Peter: Rubbish! I remember you, when you were walking along the road, and you were trying to get into the park, and you were smashing down the gate. And then when the man comes he say 'It's open, sonny, you can walk in'. Remember? You were so embarrassed, that instead of walking in the park, you walked home again, remember?

This extract is notable in that it shows a distinctly Black style of *English*, as opposed to Patois. It is perhaps impossible to draw lines of separation, but intuitively one feels that some use of English by young Black Britons is in a sense a consciously distinct Black English, while other use is an approximation to (or actually is) the local white variety used by their white peers.

Many styles of competitive (and especially more ritualistic) language do, however, seem to select for a dialect in the Creole half of the continuum – that is, Patois or something that is more Patois than English. Under this general grouping is included all the highly competitive use of language in the group situation mentioned earlier involving either noisy voice overlap, or strongly voiced confrontations, or both. Within this we can further distinguish a whole range of styles

meshing or interspersing with another. For instance, there is
the very common form of verbal duel for which we have the
community terms **cussin'** and **tauntin'** where the classic formula is **Yuh face favour X** – X being an unflattering, usually
non-human co-referent. This is verbal activity that perhaps
older adolescents find childish. (However, I have one account
of a father using it to quell his adolescent daughter – unsuc-
cessfully.)

These two boys were aged 13:

E: fi-yuh 'ead long like dem coconut.
S: Wha! Yuh favour pumpkin.
E: Yuh favour ... ackee.
S: Ackee?
E: Yuh see yuh 'ead dry [bald] like dem peel-'ead Johncrow [bald-
      headed vultures].

– and so it goes on. Often in such contests the opponents
switch to invective consisting of vivid threats, which in turn
may take on all the righteous force of parental 'cussing'
or may run more to fantasy in which just deserts will be
received.

E: A donkey give yuh two back kick yuh fly to wheh yuh come from.
S: Bwoy, if a tek a catapult, bwoy yuh betta get outa range.
E: Mi naa get outa range.
S: ... 'cos when mi ready to aim, I will lick everything offa yuh.
      One shot an' cou' peel-off. ...
E: When y'a h'aim, yuh naa aim afta mi, yuh aim afta somep'n. But
      when a'm h'aimin', mate, mi a haim afta yuh y'eye [I shall aim at
      your eye].

The use of rhymed insults is a well-known form of duelling, usually selecting the opponent's mother as the butt of
the insult. It is found in various places in the Caribbean and
also in the United States where it is incorporated into the
'woofing' or 'sounding' described by Abrahams, Labov and
others. In the data collected in Bedford in 1974 there is
surprisingly little rhyming. From that evidence one could
have concluded that unrhymed insults and threats predomi-
nated in competitive taunting and cussing. Since then,
examples of rhyming have been collected, both the traditional

Caribbean type in which set-formula rhymed couplets are used (this was recorded from a Grenadian) and the following type, which is possibly more typically Jamaican and more typical of British-born Blacks. It consists of improvised rhymed couplets introduced by **mi seh**:

> Mi seh she come from Guyana
> And she nyam off [eats up] banana.

This particular example is taken from a whole sequence produced by pupils of Steve Hoyle at Santley Junior School, Brixton (V. Edwards 1979b: 126). They improvised these after being played the rhyme: 'Mi seh she come from Jamaica, and she daddy is a baker' from a record by Dennis Alcapone. The same technique was used in a verbal duelling sequence taped at a Bedford school in 1980, where a succession of insults of this type ('yuh seh yuh head favour garden shed') overwhelmed the opposition.

Proverbs have already been mentioned in connection with mock aggressive word play. In the sample of word play below the 'storyline' seems to be that of a proverbial story or fable. (Such fables were described by one boy from a French Creole speaking background as 'jokes'.) The antics here of Fox and Monkey are also more than a little reminiscent of those in the Black American toast (rhymed story) 'The signifying Monkey'. Incidentally, in the extract, Roy is identifying with the monkey and Peter with the fox.

Peter: Monkey strikes again!
Roy: How bout yuh. Fox strikes again. Monkey ha more tricks dan fox. Fox deh try [was trying] to catch Monkey an all di Monkey do is ... jumpin' deh, jumpin' deh. Monkey does 'ooo-er' [pulls face]. Fox sat deh goin 'ooo-er'. Monkey ...
Peter: Fox is mo' cleva dan Monkey. Di Monkey deh jump, deh jump. Monkey fell down broke him backside.
Roy: Wha Fox deh walkin' nice? Fox deh walkin' nice, im fall dong eena big hole an' a see a big lion go up an' bite Fox bum-bum. An i Fox go [howls].
Peter: Mista wons Monkey deh climb di tree: budum budum! Monkey slip an' broke him backside, Fox come 'baa-ing', kick Monkey up him backside. Fi-yuh monkey fly!

IDENTITY

In the 'Afro' reaches of society amongst ordinary people, particularly in the peer group, Caribbean culture seems to have an integrity despite a perpetual 'divine discontent'. As J. Edwards *et al.* (1975) point out, the widespread Caribbean emphasis on skills of wit and performance appears to be closely interrelated with the dual value system. Thus the clash of values becomes subsumed in an Afro-Caribbean cultural theme of witty debate. Black life thrives on Blake's opposition of contraries. Creole and other African manifestations may be referred to as **bad**, but this is an ambiguous term in Black vernacular speech: **bad** frequently means **good**. (See Reisman (1970) on cultural ambiguity in Antigua, and Abrahams (1976) for discussion of this theme in Black America.) Such strategy, while it may have derived from African usage, is highly appropriate to the Caribbean situation. It enables the speakers to reduce the contradictions about their racial/cultural identity to superficiality or nothing. It is yet another example of adaptation or camouflaging, Anansi-style, so that the African values survive.

Problems arise when one moves out of the supportive 'Afro' milieu into the middle class, or into the white society of Britain. Here there is every likelihood that apparent contradictions become acutely real. The Afro cultural identity is ambiguous, submerged and largely uncodified, and it is only too easy to deny because of the very qualities that have ensured its survival up until now – its ability to conceal and adapt. Also the Black/Afro identity with its connection with slavery is highly stigmatized in mainstream white society *and* in Black middle-class society. Here, until recently, it was not even polite to say 'Black'. From the same vantage point the vernacular culture is seen as disgusting or lacking – lacking not only a history and official language, but also a recognized literature or the backing of an official education system. Add to all this a perception by many Black children that they are not going to be completely accepted by the white world, and the position for some individuals is desperate, untenable. They feel dispossessed of themselves:

...
Cry for me
You white bastard
You took my identity
SHIT ... you don't even know what I'm talking about!

Now you're going to lock me away
In some dark place for many years.
Can't you even shed one God-damn tear?
You are the ones who are dumb.
You are the ones who make us all go mad.
Can't you find it in your heart to cry a little?
Why don't you leave us alone?
Can't you see what you have done to us?
Cry nah!

[Sandra Agard, 'Cry For Me', in *Talking Blues* (1976)]

Note the use of Patois at the close, the symbol of what is denied. There must be very few people outside the Black community who appreciate the exact nuance of 'Cry nah!' It is a plea, a way of saying 'won't you cry?' or 'please cry'. It is as if there is no way of making the white man understand, and so it makes no difference if the language is opaque to him, provided that fellow Blacks understand.

The literary response: the Caribbean

John Richmond once used a telling phrase: 'crisis spawns beauty'. The crisis of identity has provoked a wide range of responses from Caribbean novelists and poets over the past twenty years or so. V. S. Naipaul explores the theme of rootlessness and psychic disintegration to its logical extreme. In one of his most significant novels, *A House for Mr Biswas* (1961), Naipaul expands beyond parochial concerns with the Hindu life of Trinidad, beyond the theme of race, and outlines the struggle to retain personality in a society that denies it. George Lamming explores a theme of lack of self-awareness, which he sees as the slave-mentality. In a group of essays *The Pleasures of Exile* (1960) there is a dialogue on the problem between Caliban (Lamming/Caribbean man) and Prospero (the white man). Lamming concludes that the two must work together in the context of a new horizon in which ' ... the psychological legacy of their original contract will have been annulled' (p. 159).

However, the most significant recent developments on this literary scene are the positive affirmations of the culture. Poet and novelist Wilson Harris seeks to celebrate the diversity as a strength. Out of the contradictions, Harris's affirmation has led to a series of novels that are exceptional in every way. In these he 'is concerned not only to redress the balance of the Caribbean schizophrenia, but also to heal the divided consciousness of Man' (Gilkes 1975: 153). His work is clearly in a class of its own. On the other hand, certain poets, notably Louise Bennett and Edward Brathwaite, have adopted the voice of the ordinary people. Brathwaite's poem 'The Dust' (1967) is especially to be regarded as a breakthrough. In this, the language and vision of the proverb, the folk song and the unexceptional West Indian man and woman become the medium of a deceptively simple poem that has almost epic overtones. From the point of view of West Indian cultures (Bajan in this case), 'The Dust' is a crucial achievement. The use of dialect, incidentally, does not render the poem inaccessible to white readers.

The response in Britain

Developments in the West Indian community of the United Kingdom are equally exciting. The quality of the literature that is now emerging is surprisingly high in view of the size of population. The explanation possibly lies in the language resources available to the community, and in the severity of the cultural dilemma.

Prose

There have been a number of short stories written and published in Britain that are partly, or wholly, in Patois. Most notable perhaps are Jennifer Johnson's *Ballad For You* and *Park Bench Blues* (1978). In these, the use of Patois as a medium is fluent and accomplished throughout. No crisis of identity is expressed, but Black ideas, qualities and deeds are more or less consciously celebrated. Perhaps it is in the nature of this genre to be less intellectually self-conscious.

In the Melting Pot (n.d.) by Chelsea Herbert is even more
relaxed, a loosely constructed uncomplicated work expressing the everyday concerns of a teenage girl, in a range of
language that could be described as London/Jamaican in
about equal proportions.

Two other notable prose works by young Jamaicans in
London are 'Mouta Massy' by Sandra Herridge (which appears
in full at the end of chapter 3) and *Jamaica Child* by Errol
O'Connor. Both these well-written pieces employ standard
English for the narrator's voice and a range of dialect for the
dialogue (in 'Mouta Massey' a deliberate tension is set up
between 'natural' Patois and standard English dialogue).
O'Connor's story is rich with the detail of everyday life in the
interior of Jamaica. It is almost a textbook on the Afro-
Jamaican culture that invests this life: there are riddles, folk
tales, folk song, superstition and folk belief. And yet the
contradictory currents in Caribbean culture are recognized:
the mother's critical remarks, for instance – 'Yu no really
believe in dem t'ings, dey?' – and the very fact that the
background narration is in standard English:

The evening sun was at the end of its day's journey, and it slowly sank
behind the mountains as it had done for centuries. Darkness came and
helped to show the beauty of the sky and the mountains and the valley.
The night was warm, the breeze was blowing gently. Many families were
out on their doorsteps or verandahs sitting and listening to the wonder-
ful noises of nature. Others were maybe just simply enjoying the stories
they were being told by their grandfathers or other older members of
the family.

I asked Papa why the sun shone in the daytime and the moon at
night. He explained it to me, but I never did understand what he was
talking about. After some time explaining, somehow he saw the dumb
look on my face. So explained it another way, the way I liked best.

'Millions an' millions of 'ears ago, when only de moon an' de sun
was about', Papa began, 'de sun an' de moon use to shine in de day time
togeda, because dey was good, good fren' den. Time go by an' de moon
became grumbly an' neva satisfied . . . like dese woman nowadays, neva
satisfied . . . anyway, de sun try an' try fe please de greedy moon, but
de moon still neva satisfi. So one deay de sun start fe quarril wid de
moon. Soon dey was fighting . . . '

'Who win?' I asked, as I smiled at the idea of the sun and the moon
fighting. ' . . . me no know, de sun a sopose . . . de sun tell de moon fe

leave, an' neva to come back. De moon gat in a temper an' lef' de place. So de sun naa talk to de moon, an' de moon naa talk to de sun. To dis day, the sun an' de moon shine different time to avoid each ada.' Papa finished with a smile on his face.

'Wa 'bout de stars den?' I asked.

'Every star in de sky, signify a person an' earth ... when one a de star drap den dat mean sumbaddy die, dem call it de fallin' star,' Papa answered.

'Yu no really believe in dem t'ings, dey?' Mama asked.

'No mus' [certainly, inevitably],' Papa answered, again.

[*Jamaica Child*, pp. 26-7]

This folk story within a story is in essence and style similar to the 'Legend of the Wind and the Water' told by Hurston (Black American, Florida) and even closer to the 'Legend of the Sun and the Moon' (Togoland and Dahomey) both quoted in Herskovits (1941: 274–5).

Poetry

The volume of West Indian poets in Britain, *Bluefoot Traveller* (1976), contains poetry that is striking in its immediacy, its dialect range and its technically successful handling of this range. James Berry (editor and contributor) is being unduly pessimistic when he writes in the introduction: 'West Indians here are a long way from the dynamic cultural activities of American blacks or their fellow West Indians at home. They are grossly under-explored, under-expressed, under-produced, and under-contributing.' While it is obvious what he means, this volume of poems itself is indicative of a potential that is at least *beginning* to be realized. Linton Kwesi Johnson is one of the most widely known of the poets. He frequently takes on 'the voice of the people', but in this case it is the angry voice of London Black youth. In poems such as 'Reggae Sounds' (in *Bluefoot Traveller*) and 'Dread Beat and Blood' the poet uses a Black English in a way that grows out of the dynamic aspects of the Caribbean voice, where the voice and the movement merge:

> Shock-black bubble-doun-beat bouncing
> rock-wise tumble-doun soun music:
> foot-drop find drum blood story;
> bass history is a moving
> is a hurting black story.

Thunder from a bass drum sounding,
lightening from a trumpet and a organ;
bass and rhythm and trumpet double-up,
team up with drums for a deep doun searching. . . .
[L. K. Johnson, 'Reggae Sounds']

This is meant for dramatic delivery. It is no surprise that this
kind of poetry merges into Jamaican music. Johnson has in
fact brought his poetry to young Black people on record,
where it becomes a kind of 'toast in'.

Even younger poets are now also finding their voices and
producing some promising work. Looking at a collection such
as *Talking Blues* (1976), several points emerge: the quality of
the work is high, the themes of identity and culture are again
explored, as well as points of friction with the white community, and the whole range of dialect is used. It is important
to realize that these young people have in a sense two verna-
culars. Where they use Patois they usually counterpoint it
with English – which ironically can be both the voice of the
poet and of Babylon (the oppressor). Hugh Boatswain's 'Cut
up Dub' combines all these features with an ironic look at
his own people and their shortfall from the Rastafarian ideal:

    . . .
    Sounds getting mellow,
    Special Brew knocked back quick,
    Tempers getting shorter,
    Voices getting louder,
    A scream,
    A jab an' a stab,
    'Humble yourselves my little ones . . . '
    No one taking notice of the music now,
    'Humble yourselves . . . '
    Bottles start bursting,
    'Oh my brothers we can . . . '
    'Cut dem up!' shout one,
    Jah Jah's children breaking each others bones.
    Knife a flash,
    Blood a run,
    My foot a fly.

Outside, the wind blows cold,
Feet shuffle quickly in the dark.
No! Don't run!
NEVER RUN IN THE DARK IN STOKE NEWINGTON!
[Hugh Boatswain, 'Cut up Dub']

But really positive affirmation of the 'Roots' culture, its strength and power, in spite of the forces ranged against it, is found only in poems that celebrate movement and beat. However labyrinthine the problem of identity on an intellectual level, resolution is possible here:

Oh Africa – Land of the Roaming Lion,
Ras-Conquering Lion of the Tribe of Judah
    celestial dub
    high bass-line riff
    strong drum beat
Pounding his soul
Like a cool breeze cutting through the high grass,
Parting them
Leaving no secret hidden
    heavy bass line
    strong drum beat
Searching, searching,
Hard Trenchtown dub rock
    yeah
                [Hugh Boatswain, 'Dub Rock']

This compares with the work of the Black American poet Langston Hughes:

My song
From the dark lips
Of Africa
Deep
As the rich earth
Beautiful
As the black night
Strong
As the first iron
Black
Out of Africa
Me and my
Song.

Concerning another poem by Hughes, Jean Wagner writes:

In this poem, Harlem and the beneficent rhythms of Harlem jazz are presented as a haven of peace for the Negro who has spent a harassing day serving white men, and this sanctuary status allotted the world of jazz is the direct consequence of the similarity between its rhythms and those of the tribal dance in the African countryside, evoked by the poem in a delicate filigree. [Wagner 1973: 409]

It is plain that 'hard' Trenchtown dub rock offers the same kind of solace to Black British youth. The celebration of this fact in form as well as in content, in 'Dread Beat and Blood', 'Dub Rock' and other poems, goes beyond mere recognition of that solace and becomes an act of cultural strength.

Wilson Harris, Ras Tafari and the Black psyche

Mention was made earlier of the remarkable work of Wilson Harris. Michael Gilkes writes:

His novels illustrate what must be considered as perhaps the most remarkable and original aspect of West Indian writing, one in which the condition of cultural and racial admixture itself becomes the 'complex womb' of a new wholeness of vision. A creative attempt is made to heal the divided psyche of Caribbean Man by looking inward, towards ' ... a theme of a living drama of conception, the conception of the human person rather than the ideology of the "broken" individual'. [1975: 3]

More than 'just' returning to the roots and celebrating the Afro-culture of the Caribbean countryside, Harris is celebrating the entire contradictory blend of the culture in literature – specifically the novel. There is another comparable response – this time actually from the people themselves – which also seeks to find an all-encompassing vision, and which has been similarly described as 'healing the Black psyche': Ras Tafari. Instead of the 'broken individual', the Rastaman celebrates the 'I-an-I' of humanity. Because Jah (or God) is seen to be within everyone, all are united and members of one another. On a television programme Professor Rex Nettlefold once described this vision as a fantastic achievement for what is still considered a sub-culture of a sub-culture. Rastafarians are drawing on resources within the society, where one can be 'one an di same but individual in every sense' (*BFY*, lines 4-5). This principle is central to various distinctive Black performance styles in music, speech and other activities:

A crucial part of the Black aesthetic involves this voice overlap and interlock effect, one by which everyone gets to do their own individual 'thing' even while contributing to the overall sense of whole. This, it seems to me is the peculiar Afro-American sense of aufheben (dramatisation of opposites), the ability to 'play a part ... while asserting one's own voice, thus being both an individual and a group member. [Abrahams 1976: 83]

Yet Black people commonly see themselves as self-seeking, manipulative and generating unnecessary conflicts amongst themselves. Both Beckwith (1929) and Abrahams mention this. Neville Moore writes that there is a need for his people to be aware that they spend too much time quarrelling amongst themselves, and that this, more than anything else, is holding them back (Moore 1980).

Rastafarianism preaches a coming together 'in peace and love' in which individualities are preserved and differences that may lead to friction can be *reasoned* over in the expectation of reaching agreement. This rationale is particularly useful in thinking about integration of Black and white in British society. Before integrating ('coming together') we need to know who we are so that we can come together as ourselves.

But Ras Tafari is more than simply a political reflex action. It is, as Nettlefold put it, a redemptive ethic achieving a level of consciousness that eschews racism, exalting man, the offspring of God, whoever he may be. Neville Moore writes:

Prejudice takes many forms in man and basically it is ignorance and the lack of understanding. So never condemn those that are, until you know within yourself that you are not. [Moore 1980: 5]

While the Rastafarian movement was born out of the particular experience of Black people, some of its followers are aware of the wider relevance of their message. Big Yout' of Reggae fame is quoted as saying:

Some of these lyrics related to a people and their environment, but that does not mean that people living in other environments won't be able to understand them. I whole relationship is to reality, God of all relation is reality, ya dig? [Davis and Simon 1979: 107]

Because of the particular emphasis of this chapter it is essential to balance the picture presented here by further reading (or by talking to Rastas). I have stressed both the literary response and the Rastafarian movement as natural outgrowths of the dynamic contradictions within the culture, and as attempts to come to terms with the damage inflicted on the psyche by the experience of slavery. One could describe this as a response to the situation within. Blacks also have to contend with the situation without: the problem of growth and fulfilment in a society that is perceived to deny or degrade the identity of its Black members. Central to the interpretations of both Cashmore (1979) and Garrison (1979) is recognition of the need to overcome the interactive negative forces within and without:

The identity of the Rastaman was at the nexus of objective and subjective realities; he conceived of a reality and located himself a specific place in that reality where he could cultivate a sense of selfhood and belongingness; where he could revive the true self. [Cashmore 1979: 141]

Both writers portray Rastas as separatist. In this section I have picked up the thread of cultural independence rather than racial separation, and this is certainly Moore's theme. Rather than try to explain Rastafarian thought any further, I conclude with the slightly abridged transcript of a talk given on the movement by Neville Moore, of the Bedford Caribbean Youth Association, as part of the series of talks 'Faces of Bedford' held at the Bedford Language and Resources Centre in 1978. Naturally he gives his own interpretation.

RAS TAFARI

Neville Moore

Well I'd like to talk about the Rastafarian movement; firstly, because you must have heard certain things, right? You must have seen people walking around – you've noticed that something's on, anyway. Now, I think the first thing, which is really important, is the fact that reasoning is something that we really look to, within the Rastafarian movement – it's like deep conversation, deep talking. If anything has come up, or, you talk about something, you have to reason out. Because, that's why, certain times, if you went to London now, some man might say something slightly different to I, picking up because of the group of people he's with. So sometimes it varies from place to place. It doesn't sort of stray too far away, that is the biggest thing, but it slightly varies a little bit.

You see some of the guys going around with a tam, a hat, on their head, and it sometimes got colours of *red gold* and *green* or red yellow and green, right? Now, that is the colours of Ras Tafari, the colours of Ethiopia, and some Rastamen say well Ethopia is like where it is now. But we say Ethiopia is AEthiopia (I-Ethiopia), the Greek term, which is 'land of the black-faced man', which is Africa, which when they said it, was Africa. So we look to that as Africa and we look to the colours of Africa, this is why some of the Rastas wear it. But then, you can't always recognise the Rastaman from the way he looks. A Rastaman ... you can't tell. You have to go and reason with the man. You must go and sort things out. You must see what that man is, before you can say he's a Rastaman. Because not all these so called Rasta are Rasta. It is difficult for you probaby to understand this but, it's like some of them are just wearing it to catch on, or to some of them it's fashion, right? Certain trends come through like the teenage punk rockers, or whatever, right? They just join on. Now most of these people just die off towards the end, or some of them get into it deeper and carry on.

Now amongst other things basically a Rastaman is a culturalist. He believes that the culture, which been diverted, should be regained, because his own identity is a

must. He must know about the things that have gone. Not
necessarily react to them in a sense like: Oh, slavery was this,
and before that, that was this. The man must reason. Now
the Rastaman would say: now look, slavery – OK slavery was
a certain English minority who was dealing in with that
particular trade. Now the thing is those same English people,
or the Spanish people, or Portuguese people that were doing
those things were an upper class, an aristocratic type of
people. Now those people were doing the same things to their
own people, and they were seeking money and they were
basically a materialistic type of person, whatever they were
dealing in was that, so the thing is, to know these things.
It is also right to know that some of the African Kings sold
slaves, they went out on whatever, running around and they
picked up slaves, and took them to the slave traders. But
there is also, we should know about when the missionaries
went over and taught the slaves this and taught them that and
there was a confusion which changed their way of life,
changed their way of thinking. Now all these things a Rastaman should know.

It's not enough to know about slavery, it's enough to dig
deeper into everything.

Also he's a *naturalist*. As far as possible he's natural as
possible. Which is one of the reasons for the hair right? We
grow it. It's like, the thing is, keep it natural. Don't do
anything right? Don't do anything to it, you must wash it,
you must keep it clean, you must oil it. You mustn't do
anything else. Now it's probably hard to understand, right?
Well it will be hard to understand, it must be, because it's
like, you act in a different way. But because it's different it
doesn't mean to say it should be ignored, because it's there,
and there's a lot of Rastas about now and it will probably
get bigger and bigger, and stronger and stronger as it goes on.
Because really the need is there, always I feel the need is
there, the need for identity. Because the thing is, there's a
lot of black youths even in Bedford – well we're talking
about Bedford because this is where we are – and they're
finding it easier to relate to us, than they are to their parents
or their school teachers, because we think basically we are
like youths that are grown up, and grown up in Bedford.

Now we know the way they feel, they come to us, they talk
to us and if we can, we give them guidance sometimes and
things like that. But the thing is, they're looking for something, right? and I feel it is an identity, they're looking for.
They're looking for an identity, in us, just something to grasp
onto, something to go forward with. It's all right saying:
'Come together, come together as one, one unity'. But if
you're going to come together you must come together, as
something. What are you? Now if an Englishman says: 'Look,
why don't we just come together?' what would I come
together as? What am I, a West Indian? Am I African? Am I
a Bedfordian? You know, they have to latch onto something.
And when they can latch onto something, then they can be
relaxed. And from when they relax they can do well. Now if
they can carry on in a relaxed manner, instead of getting all
the sidetracking coming to them say – do this, do that.

Now the parents, a lot of our parents, it's a funny situation
really, they seem to be more interested in 'A' levels and
certain exams anyway. Now to I or to a Rastaman, the thing
to do when you're teaching a youth, is to tell that youth to
do his best, a hundred per cent. If you can do your best, a
hundred per cent, then whatever results you come up with,
that is good, because you've tried your best. Now it's not
enough to sit down and say: Oh, I want you to be a lawyer.
Because this is what some of our parents say is: right, I want
you to be lawyer, I want you to be a bank manager, I want
you to be a director. Now, it's just the way things are, the
way Black people stay. Anyway it's just how we are, right?
Now, this is things our parents come to us with, this is what
they tell us, this is what they want us to be. Now, not all of
us are cut out to be these things. So, it's not on. But the
thing is, it's a lot of pressure. Now all these kids are going
there, they're a bit nervous about what results they have,
because, say, their parents are going to say this, or their
parents are going to say that. I mean in some cases some
parents a-go on and say: dem will kick dem kids out if they
don't do this or don't do that, or they got to try harder. Now
if they're trying their hardest, how can they try harder? Now,
you know, if one kid who is really intelligent goes to school
and he really comes out well, and he's not trying his best,
I feel that kid is worse than the kid that goes there, and tries

his best, and doesn't come out with anything. Because that one has done his best. He will carry on with that way, in him, the rest of his life, he will do his best, he will be doing a hundred per cent all the time, when he's out, he's doing a hundred per cent, and a hundred per cent, to me, well he's right. Because, that's what you should be doing in life, as life goes on.

Now a Rastaman also believe in natural things, right? Now a Rastaman believes that nature is the basis of life, nature is what we should be looking to, because nature has more things to offer than what certain people would think now. It's like – nature is life, anyway, and the more you recognize nature, the more you will understand yourself. And basically the doctrine is peace and love, peace, love and unity, and coming together, under one understanding. Now if you understand one another, you must come together and you must reason. This is how we stay. You must come together and you must discuss, you must discuss. You must discuss all aspects of what's going on. And don't just skim over things, or go from one extreme to another.

I hear things of, saying about bringing up the children, right? Now, the Rasta would say: look, the thing is it's not enough to say don't beat them, or one side say beat them. The thing is, in all things there is a happy medium, there is a middle of everything, right? So the thing is, a youth must be chastised. It's one of these things. You must do it. A youth must be told when to stop. You can't say: well I'm not going to hit my child, or, I'm going to beat it out of him, because they're two extremes and they're both as useless as each other. You must teach them in the middle, you must tell them, well look, you must beat them at certain times or later on. If you can hit them when they're young, if you can get them when they're young, when they get older they'll have more respect. They will understand. You will just have to tell them and they will understand straightaway.

[Neville Moore then explains how the group of Rastafarians he belongs to have set up a club in the Howard Chapel in Bedford.[2] He expresses a hope that young people who are

[2] The association have temporary accommodation there. They have applied for aid from grant-giving agencies, but have been unsuccessful up to the time of writing.

'getting into a bit of trouble here and there will come to the club to talk'.]

And not only to talk to us, we don't only want them to know of us, we want them to know of other things. Because we know they're looking but we don't want them to start on drugs, we want them arrange their minds. And we would like them to be taught certain things. We'd like them to know all the things that they want to know, and out of their suggestions we will go out and find out people who can do these things.

Other than that, at the moment the Rastafarian movement in Bedford are doing a few drawings, and writing poems and wood carvings and things, and the girls are making dresses and garments. So when we do get this place together, we have quite a few things and we'll collect them all up and we shall invite certain people, well as many people as we can, to come and see them. Because it's something that is going on but it's going on under cover at the moment and we'd like to just bring it out.

I have a poem here to finish off with and it's called I-dentity:

I-dentity

Is this life as I see it today,
Or is there somewhere a different way?
A place somewhere where I know my name,
A place where I feel the same.
A place where people don't stare,
A place where people are more aware.
But what am I looking for in all this confusion?
To I there is one conclusion,
And that is to search for my lost I-dentity.
Yes to know myself, I must find my I-dentity.

[For further reading on the Rastafarian movement, see Barrett (1977); Cashmore (1979); Garrison (1979); Owens (1977).]

CHAPTER 3

Black Children and Education

... we have abandoned the belief that it is sufficient to treat all children alike. This belief denied many of the children the opportunity to reveal skills or talents which would help them to feel a sense of success or achievement. As we now see it, the task of the school is to recognize, in much more positive ways than before, the group identity which the pupils have through their family history and their home culture. Indeed these factors are even more important in view of the position of immigrant pupils as a distinct minority group in their neighbourhood, city and in Britain generally. We now understand much more fully than ever before that a multi-racial school cannot succeed in either its educational or social aims if this is ignored. If any success is to be achieved in the community at large, success in the school community is vital. [George Meredith writing in McNeal and Rogers (1971: 103) about his experience as the head of a multi-ethnic school in the Midlands]

ADVANTAGE AND DISADVANTAGE

All the aspects of the language and culture of Black people in Britain that I have touched upon can be related to education. Strictly speaking, perhaps, a consideration of education lies outside the scope of this book. However, this chapter represents a concise, not to say terse, note on the subject, supplemented by an article by John Richmond providing practical insights.

There is some disquiet about the way West Indian children fare in British schools. The Rampton/Swann committee has been set up to inquire into the education of children from ethnic minority groups with particular reference to pupils of

West Indian origin. Rather than begin with an emphasis on problems, however, it would be useful to look at the positives in the situation. If teachers look at the distinctive cultural backgrounds of their pupils they will find strengths that can be cultivated.

Firstly, the will to succeed in school was a strong asset that West Indians brought with them into British classrooms. Respect for education is widespread and traditional in the Islands. Unfortunately, school failure is just as widespread, particularly in rural Jamaican schools, brought about by over-crowding and lack of equipment, and an educational system that up until the present has been biased against the cultural identity of the child. This is well documented in Bagley (1979: 69–72) and elsewhere. Black working-class rural Jamaicans especially came to Britain to advance themselves in social and economic terms, and they saw British education as the means by which their children could achieve these ends. McNeal and Rogers commented on this favourable factor in 1971:

Despite the difficult circumstances from which most immigrant pupils enter school, they have brought with them a positive, not to say avid, regard for education. The blight of demoralisation and apathy which affects large numbers of the English pupils in deprived schools has not yet completely enveloped immigrant pupils. This is a positive factor which ought to be used to fashion a sound educational policy. But it will continue only as long as schools seem to be providing opportunities that their pupils seek from their education. [McNeal and Rogers 1971: 22–3]

Secondly, development of confidence and fluency in speech is fostered in the culture, not only in the informal peer group setting, but in the reasoning of Ras Tafari and in various other settings, notably in the churches. Such oral fluency ought to be transferable to school work. Important potential growth points for education are narrative, drama and poetry. Martin and several other children recorded for the Bedford Survey exhibited narrative skills that could have formed a very good basis for development in written language work. The dramatic ability that I have seen demonstrated over and again has already begun to surface in school in 'Jamaican drama' – perhaps 'Brixton Blues' is the best-known example of this genre. However, fluent dramatic role-play has the potential for much wider application across the curriculum – we simply are not accustomed to using it very much, except in 'drama lessons'. Poetry is being written by the younger generation that draws on the various levels of dialect and verbal styles. This is a growing tradition inside *and* outside school, powered by an urgent need to sort out identity and position relative to mainstream society.

Thirdly, continual switching between different linguistic systems has led, as we have seen, to a heightened awareness amongst West Indians of the different linguistic levels they are using: phonology, grammatical forms and styles. Courtney Cazden (1974) suggests that this 'metalinguistic awareness' (attention to what is normally the invisible medium) forms a necessary part of learning to read. Thus bilingual and bidialectal children have an advantage in school-based language development and literacy work because of their adept focusing on language as medium. Cazden compares this ability with the skills involved in speaking 'Pig Latin'.

Despite all these positives West Indian children are not, on the whole, flourishing in British schools. In fact, there is some indication that they are doing less well than the white lower working class, the group that has always fared badly in education. It is widely observed and documented (see for instance Husén 1975: 142–57) that school failure correlates with social class and the standard/non-standard axis. The explanations advanced for this can broadly be divided into:

(1) Lack of motivation; lack of aspirations.

(2) Other environmental factors: principally lack of stimulation and mental nurture in the child's out of school life.

(3) The non-standard speech of the child, which is variously seen as less well formed than standard speech, as indicative of the child's lack of orientation towards the school culture, or (the view of most linguists) as eliciting unfavourable reactions from standard speakers who matter.

This threefold list cancels out the threefold list of strengths that I have drawn up for West Indian children. The positives have been rendered negative. The great danger is that we are allowing this to happen in the classroom.

Leaving aside the question of motivation, the thorny problem is that the school has traditionally not considered non-standard dialect and working-class culture as part of its business. So it has been a question not so much of the *indirect* influence of background on attainment, i.e. in terms of intellectual development, as of the *direct* involvement of background in that it provides forms of speech and culture that the working-class pupil cannot use without being penalized. At the same time, the chances are that if the school rejects this aspect of the child's identity then the child will reciprocate and gradually come to reject the language and culture of the school.

Despite all these damaging effects, most schools continue to prize standard English and derogate non-standard dialects. Yet no theoretical support for such a policy can be derived from linguistics. There is virtually unanimous recognition amongst linguists that one language or dialect is as good as another. Furthermore, it is possible to demonstrate that educational disadvantage is caused not by the child's background *per se*, but by society's stereotyped reaction to it. One technique that has proved particularly useful in eliciting attitudes toward particular types of language is the 'matched guise' technique. In this, tapes of the same speaker using two different language varieties are played to a panel of 'judges' (who are left to assume that they are listening to two different people). The judges then note their reactions to the voices on various scales. There have been a number of such experiments, producing quite consistent results. When using the socially less acceptable variety the speaker is seen variously as less intelligent, less attractive, less competent, even shorter! (See, for example, Lambert *et al.* 1960 – the original matched guise study of French–English bilinguals in Canada – d'Anglejan and Tucker 1973.)

Attitudes to West Indian speech in Britain have been elicited by Vivien Edwards (1976) using similar techniques. In this experiment both teachers and young West Indians viewed West Indian speakers less favourably than working- and middle-class white children. A West Indian girl who was presented speaking first with a Reading working-class accent and then with a Bajan accent was viewed more favourably in the former guise. An important finding is that these reactions are, broadly speaking, constant across groups of judges from the different language communities involved. French Canadians, for instance, were found to downgrade the French guise in the same way as the English Canadians did. Both groups had absorbed the negative stereotypes associated with the less powerful (French) community. A comprehensive, readable review of research on language attitudes, and language and disadvantage generally, is to be found in J. R. Edwards (1979).

Many teachers are very strongly aware of the necessity to start where the child is, and are working out ways of exploiting the individual child's language strengths. There are three points to be made clear, however. Firstly, the school's orientatation to standard English and non-engagement with non-standard is a firmly established tradition that runs deep. A radical reorientation of the school may be necessary if the child who says 'I ain't never gonna get nowhere at school 'cos of the way I speak' is to be allowed to prove himself wrong. A policy across the curriculum may need to be hammered out. Secondly, on an individual basis many teachers would probably have to reorientate themselves: as we have seen, prejudices towards non-standard are deeply ingrained and are absorbed by everyone. The third point specifically concerns Black children. Up until the present most teachers have been 'colour blind' on the assumption that the best way to avoid unpleasantness about race is not to draw attention to race. They have therefore not been keen to recognize differences between Blacks and others, even less make creative use of them. Far from being a convincing counter argument, this approach (or lack of one) is actually harmful in the context of the Black child's effort to come to terms with his/her own identity in a predominantly white society. The curriculum should not reinforce the difficulties by ignoring the presence of Black people, their achievements in the Caribbean, America and Africa, and their contribution to world history and culture. The Afro-Caribbean Education resources project, based in London, provides an example of the development of ways of working to redress the balance.

In the last chapter, in discussing identity, emphasis was laid on the problem within. It would be useful here to stress the problem without: the hostile society. Most teachers are white and middle class, so their subjective perceptions of race relations are likely to be quite different from those of their West Indian pupils. Teachers are somewhat insulated from the stresses (except in the classroom!) and could be characterized not unfairly as seeing racial discrimination as an occasional and isolated phenomenon. (See, for instance, 'Cause For Concern' – Black People's Progressive Association, Redbridge Community Relations Commission, 1978.) Their Black pupils, by contrast, are aware of discrimination and hostility as something that pervades the society they live in. It is difficult to make an objective assessment, but there are measures that can be used. For instance, the figures in table 3.1 show underemployment to be associated with race. The analysis of jobs of white and minority men with the same educational qualifications indicates how racial discrimination affects the employment prospects of ethnic minorities.

The schools stand in an ambiguous position here. They could be instrumental in making changes, but if they continue with a 'colour blind' policy they will be consciously defined as part of the hostile society. They will then be consciously rejected by a large section of the Black community in a way that has previously not happened. It is very important, therefore, that British schools make their position unambiguous – and this will have to involve more than a token gesture. Bagley speculates on the future, the volatile nature of the situation:

If the educational system is to meet the needs of new generations of black children it will have to change in quite fundamental ways. Such

TABLE 3.1 *Job level analysed by academic qualifications, white and minority men*

| | Men having stated qualifications as highest | | | | | |
| Job level of men in job market who have worked | Degree/prof. qualification to degree level* | | 'A' level/Asian BA/BSc | | 'O' level and equivalents | |
	White %	Minority %	White %	Minority %	White %	Minority %
Professional/ management	79	31	38	23	33	8
White collar	22	48	45	32	37	33
Skilled manual	0	14	11	27	21	37
Semi-skilled/un- skilled manual	0	7	6	18	9	22

* Excluding Asian first degrees.

Source: Urban Deprivation, Racial Inequality, and Social Policy. A Report (1977), as reported in *The Times Educational Supplement*, 13 March 1977.

change will, I anticipate, come in response to general political and social conflicts in which a vocal black community will play a major part. [Bagley 1979: 77]

A further clarification needs to be made here on the subject of race. Stereotypes associated with different ethnic and social groups are evoked not only by the language they use but also by the *way they look*. Such stereotypes affect everyone. The nettle that white educators have to grasp is that the stereotypes that inflict a feeling of inferiority on Blacks inflict the same feeling of Black inferiority on whites too, in just as pervasive a fashion! As the Redbridge survey put it, in assessing the education chances of West Indian pupils in a London borough, there is a need for teachers to come to terms with their own prejudices. The most constructive step that schools can take is to recognize the situation in which Black people in Britain find themselves, and to set about improving communications with the Black community. The importance of improving links between the home and school can hardly be over-emphasized. Black parents tend to have high aspirations for their children and yet feel cut off from the school, which leads to various negative feelings towards it ranging from mild anxiety to unalloyed bitterness.

It is plain that the issue of language remains centrally important, whether one is discussing the exploiting of cultural strengths or the need to accept the child's cultural and racial identity. This is in a sense a very hopeful aspect, because the potential for improvement in this area is great. The approach of individual teachers to Black language clearly has to be tactful and even oblique in view of the sensitivity attached to language use in general and the use of Patois in particular. However, the barriers can be dissolved easily by sympathetic teachers. Researchers and educators need to survey examples of good practice in order to provide a pool of relevant experience. V. Edwards provides descriptions of language work done by Caroline Griffen and Steven Hoyle in London classrooms (V. Edwards 1979b). (Of course there are other examples, and the reader's attention is particularly drawn to the highly beneficial collaboration between teachers working in this area and Harold Rosen and his colleagues at the London Institute of Education, under the banner of the Language in Inner City Schools movement.)

I conclude this note on education with an article by John Richmond on his work with West Indian pupils at Vauxhall Manor School, London. Richmond does not dismiss the importance of standard English, particularly in writing. He argues, however, that its acquisition could be seen as part of a general programme of language development that seeks to foster the language skills that the children possess across the wide range of dialect.

DIALECT AS PART OF THE WORK OF THE ENGLISH CLASSROOM[1]

John Richmond

My own interest in the power, beauty and subtlety of JC was largely provoked by 'Brixton Blues', an improvised play done by a third-year class of mine in September 76, which relies heavily on JC speech forms. That play caused something of a stir in the school, and provoked a range of responses, from massive enthusiasm on the part of the girls who watched the videotape, or read and acted out the transcript of the videotape, to deep suspicion on the part of some staff that this kind of thing was going on as part of the curriculum of the school. One of the play's most creative effects, in my view, was that it set the precedent that this very important area of the language range of many of the children was actually admitted to exist in one small corner of one subject of the secondary curriculum. The play started a tradition of dialect plays, poems and stories in English lessons. We didn't make a great fuss of it. No one was ever forced to write in dialect, though I have several times been accused of 'teaching these children patois'. It was simply known that those who wanted to, and knew how to, use dialect as part of their English work, were welcome to.

Here are two examples of the tradition. The poem is by Julie Roberts, the story by Sandra Herridge.

No Justice

We nah get justice inna dis ya
Babylon,
We h'affee seek ah justice outta
Babylon,
We mus' return to Africa our
righteous blessed land,

[1] The full version of this article appeared in *The English Magazine* in 1979. John Richmond, incidentally, is involved in projects on Language in Inner City Schools, and the work he describes here forms an integral part of his involvement. It is interesting to note that one of the girls in 'Brixton Blues' has gained a place at Cambridge.

Cause Babylonians present system
ah get way outta han',
Dem always accusing we fah wat
we nevva don'
Trying fe teach WE! right fram
wrang,
We tell dem seh we innocent
but deh dou't our word,
Dem tek us inna court an'
mek we look absurd,
We try tell dem seh Rasta no tief,
But dey dou't us still, dem
still don't beleev!

Mouta Massey

It was the day when the Common Entrance Examination results were coming out. Most of the people in Sherwood were hurrying to the Post Office to buy a newspaper.

Miss May flicked the latch of her gate, stole a last glance at herself through the glass of her bedroom window and then started her way to Sherwood crossroads, where the Post Office was. On her way there she met Miss Maty, one of Sherwood's commonest chatter boxes.

Unlike Miss May, who was well spoken and who looked quite neat, Miss Maty mixed her English with her own Jamaican way of speaking. She was wearing a pink roll-sleeve blouse, a yellow pleated skirt, that had banana stain all over the front, and a kata on her head. She was carrying a bucket of water, but when she saw Miss May she put it down on the roadside, leaving only the kata on her head. She was preparing to gossip.

People in the district teased her by saying that the quickest way to spread news around the place was to tell Miss Maty. Because of her great liking to exercise her lips, they nicknamed her 'Mouta Massey'.

Her excuse for being so nosey was that she lived all by herself and so, when she gets an opportunity to gossip there wasn't any harm in that. But the gossiping lips of Miss Maty often got her in difficult situations. That morning when she met Miss May was one of the many occasions.

Miss May: Good morning Miss Maty, how are you this morning?
Miss Maty: Mi aright May. Wey yuh going?
Miss May: I'm just going to the Post Office to buy a glena.
Miss Maty: Eh! eh! Yuh ton big shot ova night. Is only backra reading glena nowadays.

Miss May: Don't be like that Miss Maty, I'm a working woman and I have all the rights in the world to read the papers when I want to!

Miss Maty: Sarry Miss May, but mi neva know dat yuh read al papers. Mi shoudve guessed – anyway, yuh are de posh type, only chat like mi when yuh angry.

Miss May: I don't always read the papers, but today is special, you know, the results of the Common Entrance exam are coming out. I wonder if Sonia passed? She worked hard and the teacher told me that she have a good chance.

Miss Maty: Tek mi advice, if shi pass nuh mek she goh to the same school as Jeanie gal Donna. Mi hear dat she bright in har lessons, but she don't have any manners whatsoever. Your pickney will have a good chance as long as shi nuh mingle wid dat gal. All shi tink about is ramping an' enjoying harself. An' har poor Muma, boy, sometimes mi heart grief fi de woman. Yuh know har pregnant sister was like dat. Every single night ena row shi used to go dance hall, an' stay till late. An' what about Jeanie's sister? Mi hear dat shi runnaway from home ... An' ... an' ...

Miss May: Aright! Aright!!! Aright Miss Maty. Yuh making yuh mouth fly like cabbage ena pat! Cho man! people dont have no secret in disa place. Yuh know more bout people's background than dem know demselves. I don't have time to labrish wid yuh! Mi gane!

Miss Maty: Wait fi mi! Mi deh com wid yuh!

Miss May: I do not wish to talk or walk with you Miss Maty. All a person need to lose their dignity is a bit of your lips, and anyway I haven't got time to wait until you go home and change.

Miss Maty: But mi not going home, mi coming like this.

Miss May: What?! People don't go to Sherwood crossroads like that!

Miss Maty: But mi not going to Sherwood crossroads. Mi will turn back half way, mi upset yuh, so mi will come and just keep yuh company.

Miss May: It's really nice of you Miss Maty, but you really don't have to.

Miss Maty: But I want to Miss May.

It wasn't until that moment that Miss May looked down. 'What are you going to do with the bucket? Miss Maty! look at your feet! Them dying to wash! You can't come to Sherwood crossroads like that surely. Look how the mud peeping from between your toes like peeping tam.'

'Oh no! I forgot to wash off mi feet. Mi slipped in a puddle when mi was helping up the bucket,' said Miss Maty.

A sudden, but somehow splendid idea flashed into Miss Maty's head. She ran to a nearby banana tree, tore a dry banana leaf from it and used the water from the bucket, with the leaf, to wash her muddy feet.

She followed behind Miss May, telling her how sorry she was for making her lose her temper. She told Miss May that when she was a little girl her mother used to give her pepper and rice to stop her from chatting so much. Then she suddenly confessed that what she told Miss May about Miss Jeanie's daughter wasn't positively true. 'Mi tink Melva tell mi, mi not sure, but yuh know she don't like Jeanie already. They did fight at pipeside an' tore off each other's blouses. It was a shame to see two grown women going on like dat. Mind yuh, mi wasn't there. I went to market, but from what I heard it was disgraceful,' remarked Miss Maty.

'Miss Maty, your lips are drifting again. If Jeanie and Melva had a fight, that's none of your business! No wonder people call you "Mouta Massy". Anyway, we soon reach Sherwood crossroads, aren't you turning back?' asked Miss May. 'Mi reach too far already, soh I might as well come all the way. Mi will go an' visit Miss Margaret, we haven't chat fi ages,' answered Miss Maty.

When they reached Sherwood Content (another name for the crossroads) Miss May went to get the newspaper and Miss Maty wandered off to gossip with a group of women whose daughters failed the exam. She talked and talked; one by one the people were leaving. Before long Miss Maty was standing barefooted, alone and sad on the piping hot Post Office step.

Miss May was nowhere to be seen so Miss Maty went home sadly.

Sonia did pass the exam and so did Donna. They were both sent to a nearby school in Falmouth. Both Miss May and Miss Jeannie were very proud of their daughters. As for Miss Maty, she continued to be a gossiper and found herself in many other embarrassing situations.

The End

THE INTERVENTION OF NON-STANDARD GRAMMAR IN MAINSTREAM SCHOOL WRITING

I come now to a more complicated question, and one which is separate from the matter of the conscious use and enjoyment of dialect as part of the work of some children, principally in English classes. In spite of what I've said, and believe to be true, about the crucial importance of accepting and encouraging children's language as it is, the fact remains that the whole state education system, and the secondary curriculum in particular, is predicated on British SE. That assumption works from the cradle at 5, to – often – the grave at 16. This puts sensitive teachers into a terrible dilemma, and I include here not just teachers of West Indian children, but teachers of all children whose language differs from the prestige dialect in which textbooks are written, which teachers for the most part use themselves, and by which children's whole lives and futures will be judged in public examinations. How do you satisfy these implacable demands, combined often with the demands of parents and of children themselves to be taught to write the language which is the key to success in this society, and at the same time maintain one's belief that the acceptance of the child's language is both ideologically desirable and pragmatically essential?

First of all we need to dispose of one generalization which is both unhelpful and untrue.

That is, that children always write the way they talk. They don't. There are plenty of children (just as, I expect, there are plenty of readers of this for whom it was true when they were at school) who move from the language they normally speak and possibly think in, to the language which they shrewdly regard as appropriate for school writing. It's called code-switching, and a lot of children do it without any trouble, do it unconsciously.

However, there are other children, I believe the majority, for whom code-switching constitutes a problem, an obstacle, a barrier to success. Somehow, every time they do a piece of writing for a teacher, it comes back covered in impatient red marks. That's very discouraging for them. It's also discouraging and irritating for the hard-worked teacher, conscientiously marking the writing, to find the same 'mistakes' cropping up again and again. Why does it happen?

Let's look at a piece of writing done for me by Pat Cummings two years ago, when she was in one of my third-year English classes. The important thing to know about Pat is that she's always been extremely school-motivated. She came into the first year of the school in 1974, finding that reading and writing were hard and problematical activities. She's in

her fifth year now and many, though not all, of her problems
have been solved. That has happened largely through her own
determination. She's never been interested in dialect writing.
In the piece which follows we see a second-generation Jamaican
girl, aged 14, writing for teacher. The piece is reproduced
exactly as I first received it from her.

At Night Club

One night I was invited to a night club with some of My friends. At
11.00 I got ready to go to the night club. My friends boyfriend pick me
up. We got to the night club at 11.30. My friends boyfriend pour me
a glass of sherry and left me all by myself. I stood around doing nothing,
no one ask me for a dance I go so board that I went outside to get some
freshair and came back in. later on I went into the changing to get
ready to go home. I open the changing room door and I left it open,
then suddenly door slammed so hard that it frightened the life out of
me. I felt so scared, I didn't want to go in the hall and asked Someone
to stay with me, because it might sound stupid for me to asked. I stayed
and went to the mirror to put some powder on my face, and as I was
putting some powder on my face I felt a Black shadow coming up to
me than all of a sudden the window slam I felt so scared that I started
to scream. Then a girl came in and calm me down. I was so scared that
couldn't open my mouth 15 mintues later I felt much better so I told
the girl my story. When I was finish what I was saying to her. She told
me that there was a young girl who died in this changing room. She said
to me the girl was only in the changing room for 15 minutes 'was she a
nice girl?' She was all right I didn't know her much. I wonder why she
wants to haunt this place.' don't aske me because I don't nothing.'
how did you feel when the Black Shadow was coming up to you'
I felt as if someone was coming up to me and lean their hand on to me.
I felt funny inside of my body' I think you do not want to say no more
about' don't you think you go home' I think I better I hope we meet
again.' 'Mary where is tom' 'we've been looking for you what have you
been it's a long story let's get in the car and I will tell you all about it.

The teacher's reaction to a piece of writing like this should
be: how do I offer practical help with this? Technically,
there's quite a lot wrong with it. Responses like 'slovenly',
'careless', which are always unhelpful, are particularly inappropriate here. The story was offered in earnest good faith.

One valid response, it occurred to me, which might help
Pat and me, would be to make an organized list of all the

features in the writing which I might want to comment on, or correct, or bear in mind for future comment and correction. I did this, and it immediately and permanently became clear that never again could I do a blanket correcting job on a pupil's writing as if all 'mistakes' came from the same source and could be treated in the same way. To begin with, those features normally regarded as straightforward errors divided quite definitely into mis-takes in the strict sense, where Pat knew what was correct but hadn't managed to transfer that knowledge accurately to the page, and examples of lack of proficiency in certain written conventions which mature writers generally regard as being useful. Presumably that distinction (represented by sections A and B in the list below) implies a different kind of handling on the part of the teacher who wants to make a helpful response. More importantly from the point of view of this article, I found that Pat was producing features in her writing which represented the grammars of non-standard dialects which, quite properly, form a part of her language competence. I use the plural 'grammars' and 'dialects' because 3 of section C is more likely to be a London vernacular influence than a JC influence. Here is the organized list I made. I'm afraid that it may seem to some readers to be stating the obvious, but I console myself with the thought that two years ago the list, once made, together with its implications, were a revelation to me.

A   Mistakes in 'At the Night Club'

(1) Misspellings: 'board'/'bored'
                      'mintues'/'minutes'
                      'aske'/'ask'

(2) Omissions: 'into the changing (room) to get ready'
                      'that (I) couldn't open my mouth'
                      'I don't (know) nothing'
                      'say no more about (it)'
                      'don't you think you (should) go home'
                      'what have you been (doing).

B   Examples of lack of proficiency in written conventions generally accepted as being useful:

(1) Omission of full stops: e.g. 'Then a girl came in and calm me down. I was so scared that (I) couldn't open my mouth 15 minutes later ... '

(2) Omission of capital letter at beginning of sentence: e.g. ' ... came back in. later on ... '

(3) Omission of apostrophe: e.g. 'My friends boyfriend'.

(4) Omission of speech marks: e.g. 'She was all right I didn't know her much. I wonder why she wants to haunt this place"' (These two sentences are spoken by different people.)

(5) Omission of question mark: e.g. 'don't you think you (should) go home'

C   Examples of dialect features:

(1) Non-use of SE -ed inflection to signal simple past; use of context or temporal phrase:
  (a) 'My friends boyfriend pick me up'
  (b) 'My friends boyfriend pour me a glass'
  (c) 'No one ask me for a dance'
  (d) 'I open the changing room door'
  (e) 'all of a sudden the window slam'
  (f) 'a girl came in and calm me down'; the standard irregular past form is used (correctly), but the present is maintained with 'calm', which has a regular past form.

(2) Use of generalized singular noun form in plural sense:
  (a) 'With some of my friend' (SE – 'friends')

(3) Use of a double negative:
  (a) 'I think you do not want to say no more about (it)'

D   Examples of features which may be related to dialect:

(1) 'I didn't want to go in the hall and asked someone to stay with me, because it might sound stupid for me to asked.' Pat would never use 'asked' in either of these contexts in speech; they are not natural dialect features at all. They seem to be an overreaction to an awareness that the '-ed' verb ending represents a frequently occurring distinction between vernacular speech and school writing.

(2) 'was coming up to me and lean their hand on to me'; it might be argued that 'lean' and the omission of '-ing' is an inconsistency unrelated to dialect. It is possible, however, that a preference for the simple present to the '-ing' form in Pat's speech means that the distance between 'was' and 'lean' has caused her to revert to the simple form; i.e. 'was' is not powerful enough to influence 'lean' at that distance.

I think Pat's position here is a very common one. There are many Jamaican, Caribbean, and for that matter indigenous London, Birmingham or Newcastle speakers, who to a greater or lesser extent than Pat are representing the grammars involved in the language they speak, in their writing. One of those grammars is SE, of course. It's foolish to say that Pat is being inconsistent because she sometimes puts -ed on the end of past tense verbs and sometimes doesn't. You wouldn't expect her to be 'consistent', given the variety of linguistic influences on her, or, to take the other sociolinguistic view, given that inherent variability is an element of the dialects of all of us.

A NECESSARY MYTH AND A POSSIBLE STRATEGY

What do I think should be done about it? My opinion divides into two sections, plan A and plan B. Plan A is cloud-cuckoo-ish and Utopian, but worth mentioning nevertheless. Given that all linguists agree that all dialects of English are equally efficient, complex and rule-governed systems, and given that we now understand the historical reasons why the prestige dialect misleadingly known as SE has achieved its dominant position, the public examination boards, universities and other arbiters of linguistic and academic standards should simply cease to penalize pupils and students who represent, in their writing, features of the non-standard grammars in the language they speak. If the will existed for that to happen, it could happen very quickly, and it would be a radical change indeed. It would certainly make our lives as teachers, and the lives of our pupils, easier and more successful than they are at the moment. It would probably raise academic

standards generally, since teachers and learners would have
more time and energy to really engage with knowledge rather
than tilt at windmills of standard and non-standard features
in writing.

However, I'm aware that we don't live in the world of
plan A, and that the educational wind at the moment is blowing away from rather than towards that world. I'm also aware
that plan B, the plan for the real world, is a compromise, and
less than satisfactory in a number of respects. But I think it's
the best we shall manage.

The first thing is that there should be a policy, understood
and agreed by all the staff in the school, on dialect features in
writing. The way to decide on and implement that policy will
vary from school to school, but a way of starting might be to
collect examples of writing done by several pupils across a
range of subjects, and analyse them in a similar fashion to
what I did with Pat's piece. The ideal group to do that would
themselves represent several major areas of the curriculum.

I'm going to stick my neck out and say what I think that
policy should be. Readers may disagree with me about the
emphasis, the tone of voice, or perhaps the timing of what I
suggest, but I hope the principle will be recognized. I believe
that up to the end of the third year in secondary school,
teachers should not attempt to standardize non-standard
features in children's writing. That, of course, assumes that
teachers know the difference between a non-standard feature
and a mistake in the first place. The damage done to children's
confidence and fluency as writers by the early and sometimes
constant rejection of their language is considerable. And
however kind or sensitive the teacher may be, I think it's
unfair to ask most children below the age of 14 to perform
such an abstraction which most middle-class children are
never called upon to perform. Up to the end of the third year
in secondary school, there's plenty to work on in helping
children to improve their writing in ways not related to
dialect.

In the fourth and fifth years of secondary school, if it's
obvious that some children are producing non-standard
features in their writing for which they will be penalized in
examinations, teachers should point out to them, preferably

individually and at the most in small groups, what those features are, and what their standard equivalents are. That's also the time when work on dialect as such can be most useful and enjoyable, and link in with advice of this kind. It may well be that the specific features in question are rather few in number. The task is often not as frightening as it sounds; 15- and 16-year-old children are increasingly making self-reflective judgements, and many of them will see the short-term sense of the advice as regards the exams.

I'm not happy with the previous paragraph. In some ways it's a shoddy compromise. But in the extremely imperfect educational world where we work, we have to avoid brutality and ignorance on the one hand, and (too much) star-gazing on the other.

Thanks to Julie Roberts, Sandra Herridge and Pat Cummings for allowing me to quote from their writings.

FURTHER SOURCES OF INFORMATION

Afro-Caribbean Education Resource Project: Resource and Information booklet. Obtainable from ACER Project, 275 Kennington Lane, London SE11 5QZ.
Caribbean Resources Guide. Obtainable from The Resources Unit, English Language and Resources Centre, Acacia Road, Bedford.

PART II

Linguistic Aspects

CHAPTER 4

British Jamaican Creole:
A Brief Analysis

The account of London-sited Jamaican Creole (JC) that follows can in no way be described as comprehensive, though it does cover, briefly, many of the major features. What this should provide is some insight into the way the language works, and some illustration of its systematicity. I shall, incidentally, look at African parallels for two of these features. Other English-based Caribbean Creoles differ in detail but show fundamentally the same grammatical system (with one or two exceptions to this noted in the text). Most of the examples given in this chapter have been drawn from Jennifer Johnson's *Ballad For You*, so that their use may be seen in context. *Ballad For You* appears in full at the end of chapter 1.

The noun

JC nouns can be definite, much as in English. Definite nouns (other than proper nouns) are preceded by the definite article *di* (= the):

> **di** biggest mout' in **di** world [*Ballad For You* (*BFY*) lines 39–40]

Nouns preceded by the possessive pronouns *mi* (my), *yu* (your), *im* (his/her/its), and so on are also definite. If the speaker wishes to indicate the plural definite, *-dem* is added to the singular definite form, after the noun. This *-dem* particle is optional, but very frequently expressed:

di addah gal-**dem** [*BFY* line 20]

dem a mi spar-**dem**.
(They are my friends.)

Obviously enough, abstract nouns and mass nouns may not
show plurality. This is similar to English where 'many breads'
and 'many braveries' are possible but awkward or marginal.
A peculiarity of Creoles is that proper nouns can, if they are
names of people, take what is known as an associative plural.
Thus:

Amarjit-**dem**
[Amarjit and her gang/team]

The reference of this Black British example was to a rounders
team captained by Amarjit.

Only count nouns (shoes, ships, cabbages and kings, but
not sealing wax) can be indefinite and singular. This is true
for both English and JC. They are then preceded by the
article *wan* or *a*:

But **one** certain set start pass remark an' a stare pan
dem. [lines 137–9]

Man, I nevah see **a** woman beat her daughter soh
in all my life. [lines 231–3]

Wá(á)n is also used to give added weight to an exclamation:

Well di satdey nite com an' is **one piece a t'ing
gwaan**. [lines 122–3]

In Sranan too you find emphatic sentences like:

mi nyan **wan aleesi**!
(That was lovely rice! – literally: I ate one/a rice!)

– which suggests that the Creole emphatic use of *wan* dates
back to the seventeenth century and the early, seemingly
common origins of the Creoles. (Of course, it is possible to
use **one** as an emphatic in American English too: 'that was
one beautiful lady!' However, this usage strikes me as quite
untypical of British English, suggesting that the Americanism
may be derived from Black usage.)

Indefinite nouns are made plural by the use of a ~~
such as *som*, *nof* (many), *plenti* or a numeral.

Nouns can be generic and in this case they need no ~
ing article. The absence of the article is indicated by φ
morpheme). Such nouns refer to generalities rather ι ιn
specific items:

> ... when dem sit down ina φ corner a chat φ people
> business ... [lines 12–13]

> You what? φ Man? You have φ man? Gal ... [line
> 222]

In this last example the generic **man** refers to men in general
as well as one man in particular, so it is neither singular nor
plural.

Personal pronouns

The system of personal pronouns typical of extreme JC are

	singular		plural
1	*mi, a* (subject)	1	*wi*
2	*yu*	2	*unu*
3	*im*	3	*dem*
	i (neuter)		

The third person *im* can be used for masculine, feminine and
neuter. All the forms (except *a*) can be used for subjective
and objective cases, and for the possessive.

JC also has special possessive pronoun forms: *fi-mi* (my),
fi-yu (your), and so on, and these are often used to emphasize
or contrast. There are several examples in *BFY*:

> ... a mek **fi dem** an' **fi him** eye mek four. [lines
> 111–12]
> (making *their* eyes and *his* eyes 'make four')

Less broad JC has feminine pronouns *shi* (subjective), *har*
(objective and possessive), *fi-har* (possessive). The *shi* objective and possessive forms that Jennifer Johnson and many
other British Black people also use are much more typical of
the Eastern Caribbean than Jamaica.[1] Interestingly, although

[1] Personal communication from Pauline Christie. Also confirmed by
Jamaican speakers in Bedford.

Jamaican Creole dominates the other Creoles in this country, Eastern Caribbean Creole forms may be filtering into the speech of those who feel sure that they are speaking Jamaican.

The verb system

Stem forms

The basic verb in JC is the stem form. In the case of action verbs ('run', 'tell', 'make', 'say' – most verbs, in fact) this expresses the past tense, or, more accurately, the English simple past and perfect tenses:

> Lightening, Chalice, Charlie an' Granny Roach
> **arrive** 'bout twelve o'clock an', as dem **step** in all
> di man dem ina di room **lef'** whey dem a dhu
> [left what they were doing] . . . [lines 127–31]

Like all Jamaican verb forms it does not add endings to indicate person. In other words it is: *mi step*, *yu step*, *im step*, and so on. Most often this stem form looks like an English present, though **lef'** in the above sentence, and a few others, resemble past tenses.

However, some verbs behave differently. They express states of mind and other states and indicate the present tense with their stem forms:

> . . . all oonu **know** is fi fight an' get on like bad
> woman. [lines 194–6]

Many of these stative verbs in JC are 'adjective-like' and correspond to adjectives or past participles in standard English:

> . . . because when dem gal **dress**, dem **sharp**. [lines
> 132–4]
> (when those girls **are dressed**, they're **sharp**)

It is hard for speakers of standard English to accept that these really are verbs, but in most respects this is what they are. They can, for instance, be marked for future tense: *wi shaap*, or past tense: *did shaap*. They can even be made progressive as in

dem gal **a sharp**.
(Those girls are getting sharp – literally: Those girls
   are sharping.)

– but this seems quite rare.

The negative
JC veibs are rendered into the negative by inserting the
negative particle (most commonly *no*, but there are other
forms) before the verb:

> ... she decide seh she **noh** want it any more. [lines
>   94–5]

For emphasis, double or multiple negatives are often used
('she decide seh she **noh** want **none no** more'). There are
exceptions to the rule to insert negative before the verb.
The modals (see glossary of linguistic terms), for instance,
pattern their negatives on coloquial English lines:

modal	*negative modal*
mosa (must)	mosn
maita (might)	maitn
kyan (can)	kyaan
kuda (could)	kudn
shuda (should)	shudn
wi (will)	wuont
wuda (would)	wudn

There is a rhetorical use of the negative in sentences that have
a positive meaning, and in this case the negative particle is
always *no* and always precedes any verb:

> **Noh** di vicar! [line 107]
> (The vicar himself!)

> mi **no** kyan bathe miself!
> (I can wash myself!)

Tense and aspect
Tense is indicated much less frequently in Atlantic Creoles
than in characteristic European languages. However, the basic
JC verb can be marked for tense by putting *ben* (or a variant

such as *en*, *wen*) before it (compare Sranan, which uses *ben* in the same way). This expresses a pluperfect meaning for an action verb, and a simple past tense (descriptive of a past state of affairs) in the case of a stative verb (a verb describing a state).

> *If mi **ben waak** huom* ... [action verb]
> (If I had walked home ...)

> *mi **ben lov** yu*. [stative verb]
> (I loved you.)

It seems that *ben* is rare in the speech of British-born Black people. They usually replace it by *did* or *woz*. There are several instances of this in *BFY*.

Aspect seems to be more important than tense in JC – that is, the marking of duration, intensity, completion, frequency and so on, of verbs.

(1) The progressive aspect (English 'is doing'/'was doing', etc.) is expressed by **a** + stem.

> Whey you **a dhu** out yah? [lines 214–15]
> (What are you doing out here?)

It can also act in the same way as an English present participle:

> ...a noh eleven o'clock you goh a you bed, an'
> now mi see you a road **a fight**. [lines 208–10]
> (It wasn't eleven o'clock that you went to bed and
> now I see you in the road fighting!)

The negative of this progressive form is not *no* + *a* + stem (as you might expect) but *naa* + stem, a form that often has a future meaning:

> Dem **naw** pay fi doze. [lines 89–90]
> (They aren't paying/aren't going to pay for those.)

(2) The habitual aspect expresses a repeated or customary action and is shown by *doz* + stem in many English-based Caribbean Creoles. In Jamaican, however, this is usually expressed simply by the stem form alone:

> ... dis jibe always **reach** Sheila.
> 1st person: 'Is whey y'u **live**, gal?'

Sheila: 'Norwood Park, man; di bench pan top a
di hill.' [Johnson, *Park Bench Blues*, penultimate
paragraph]

In Bajan, on the other hand, that would be:

... dis jibe **does always reach** Sheila.
Is where you **does live**, gal?'

(3) Completive aspect in JC is marked by *don* + stem or
stem + *don*. and indicates that an action has been completed.
Very often it can be translated as the English perfect with
has or **has just**. This does not occur in *BFY* or *Park Bench
Blues* but it does appear in the play 'Brixton Blues' (in Richmond 1977):

mi jus' a **done** tell me two pickney dem seh lang
time mi no see unna. [line 173]
(I've just finished telling my two children that
I haven't seen you (plural) for a long time.)

Of course, this is extremely common in Black American too,
and has infiltrated into white American dialects. In Haitian
(French) Creole the completive aspect marker is **fin**:

M-**fin** pale: J'ai dit. [Sylvain 1936: 92]

(4) Future aspect in JC is marked by *wi* or *go* + stem if the
reference is at all hypothetical:

Mind you, if you ask dem parents if dem is fi dem
pickney, dem **will** let you know seh dem never
seen dem before in a dem life. [lines 66–70]

The negative of this form is not *no wi*, but *wuon* (won't).
If the reference to the future is one of firm prediction or
intention then *a go* + stem is more usual. This neatly trans-
lates as 'is going to'. In negative future references it is also
possible to use the negative progressive form as noted above.

Copulas
There are many other systematic features of the language
that could be singled out as un-English. Staying with the verb
system, there is the range of 'copulas' that JC uses. These are

the monosyllables that have no meaning in themselves but that act as a link between subject and predicate. In English this means the verb **to be**: I **am** Bulgarian, the pineapple **is** juicy, the cat **is** in the car, and so on. Jamaican has a selection of different copulas/**be** forms depending on the predicate it introduces.

Be before adjectives:
Adjectives in Creole behave like verbs, as we have seen, and so in broad JC we find *im shaap* rather than *im iz shaap*. However, when the adjective is not expressed but merely understood or unknown, verb 'to be' forms are needed, and these take the form of *stan/tan* or *steh*:

> Tank God my daughter noh **stay** like oonu . . . [lines 196–7]
> (Thank God my daughter is not – 'bad' understood – like you lot.)

So when a group of young Black Bedfordians asked me to play back a tape 'to hear how our voices **stand**', they were using this piece of Creole grammar in their English dialect.

Be as an equals sign:
An equivalent of the verb 'to be' is seldom omitted in Creole before a noun (or pronoun) and here it takes the form *a* or *iz*: *Dem iz rastaman*. The narrator in *BFY* always uses *iz*:

> Now Chalice **is** di top bitch . . . [lines 157–8]

Emphasis:
A very common stylistic ploy in JC is to turn sentences round in order to shift the emphasis; rather in the same way that we say 'warm beer he couldn't abide' in English. JC sentence structure requires such sentences to be introduced by *a* or *iz*: *iz inglish im a taak* (he's talking English). As we have seen *BFY* has:

> **a** noh eleven o'clock you goh a you bed . . . [lines 208–9]
> (It wasn't eleven o'clock you went to your bed . . .)

It is important to note that JC does not invert word order for questions, so inversion is purely for emphasis.

The serial verb chain
In joining a series of verbs together JC can use *an* (and) as in
'come and join us', or it can use *fi*, which looks like the
equivalent of 'to' in English:

> Well, while dem a wait **fi** pay, Granny decide **fi**
> start eat she buns ... [lines 91–3]

Notice, however, that 'start' and 'eat' in this example are
placed end on without a *fi*. Verbs of starting, stopping and
moving especially can be strung together with other verbs
without a joining word in this way:

> Dat will teach dat gal fi **come try mash up** my
> scene ... [lines 239–40]

Often the last verb in a series will be *kom* or *go* indicating
direction. For example *kyari kom* and *kyari go* meaning
'bring' and 'take away' respectively as in:

> **Carry** mi ackee **go** a Linstead Market.

Most serial verb constructions are quite un-English. However,
a similar set of constructions is found in a very large number
of African languages. In Yoruba, for instance, you find:

> wọ́n ti mú owó wá.
> (They have taken the money come.)

> ó ń fi ọbẹ ge iṣu.
> (He is taking the knife cut yam.)

And Ibo:

> há sò anyị gáá Ábá
> (They accompany us go to Aba.)

A special case of two verbs in a serial verb chain is when
the second verb is *se* (say):

> ... dem will let you **know seh** dem never seen dem
> before in a dem life. [lines 68–70]
> (They will let you know that ...)

You can find a remnant of this usage – where **seh** is the
equivalent of English 'that' or 'quote' – in Black American
vernacular in the United States:

So Jesus tell him say 'This aint no jive'.
(So Jesus told him, 'This is genuine'.)

The word for 'say' is used in the same way in many African languages, including Twi, Ibo, Mende, Mandinka, Ewe and Kikongo. In Twi the actual word used is sɛ, and in Ibo se. This African word then has survived into modern Creoles because of a coincidence between three languages. It is commonly used even in very English-seeming language in a way that no standard English speaker would normally notice – and often still with the pronunciation *se*:

> And then again you can't say that, you can't go to your friend **say** 'Talk proper English,' because you don't even know what proper English really means yourself. [Angela C. in Richmond 1978]

Iteration
Repetition of verbs and adverbs for special effect is another feature that occurs in Black speech throughout the New World. Repetition is used in this way in English too occasionally, but never without a linking **and**, which is the case in Creoles and also in African languages. Thus a Jamaican living in Bedford described his rough treatment of cats who tried to eat the birds that he was keeping in cages:

> an catch the cat, an we beat the cat, we beat dem,
>   we beat dem, we beat dem, we beat dem, we tie
>   dem up an we beat dem.

In *BFY* we find no repetition on this scale but there is one example of repetition of an adverb in order to emphasize:

> an' is dem a control di middle a di room an' a rave **strong, strong.** [lines 156–7]

JC also abounds with a closely connected feature – reduplication or doubling of a word to create a new item of vocabulary: short hair is described as *piki-piki*, grass that has been worn by people treading as *pachi-pachi*, and reggae used to be *rege-rege* before it came to mean an internationally known type of music. These double words usually imply a drawing-out or intensifying of the original meaning so that *was-was* means 'a swarm of wasps', *wan-wan* means 'one here, one there, scattered', and *difran-difran* means 'all kinds of different'. In *BFY* there is *mash-mash*:

> Granny Roach is jus' four feet an' **mash-mash**, but
> bwoy she have di biggest mout' in di world.
> [lines 38–40]
> (Granny Roach is just four feet odd ...)

Reduplicated forms are to be found in most if not all Niger Congo languages and are also typical of Pidgins and Creoles.

That concludes the brief sketch of the grammar. The second half of this chapter, on the phonology, is included mainly for reference.

THE PHONOLOGY

On this level – the pronunciation of words – JC behaves like a dialect of English. Most of the words come from English but sound different, and sometimes very different. Every word of the last sentence, for instance, could be said as a JC word, but in that case **word** would become *wod* and **sound** would become *soun* or *song*. However, a great many words that do not rhyme in English rhyme in Creole (and, to some extent, vice versa).

Vowels

Non-standard dialects of English, be they Belfast, Appalachian or Jamaican, are very difficult for outsiders to understand until they have become 'attuned' – and what they have to attune themselves to is a different way of sorting words into groups with the same vowel sounds. Take the verse

> Rain a-come, win' a-blow.
> Chicken botty deh a-door.
> (The rain is coming, the wind is blowing.
> Chicken's rumps are outdoors.)

In JC **blow** (*bluo*) and **door** (*duo*) rhyme.[2] On the other hand **blow** (*bluo*) does not rhyme with **so** (*so*), and **door** (*duo*) does not rhyme with **jaw** (*jaa*) and **jaw** in turn only sometimes rhymes with **for** which is either *fi* or *faa* depending on the context! All the main sound changes are shown in figure 4.1, which illustrates the differences in pronunciation between standard British English (SBE) and JC in diagrammatic form. On the right are the JC vowel sounds embodied in words from *Ballad For You* (in the spelling used in the story), followed by the sounds spelt according to the system devised by Cassidy and Le Page, the compilers of the *Dictionary of Jamaican English* (adopted by Beryl Bailey and other linguists who have worked on JC, but not used ordinarily by Jamaicans writing in their own dialect). On the left are equivalent words in English, grouped according to the English pronunciation of sounds within them.

Some words show changes that do not fit with the change-over pattern of figure 4.1:

SBE			*JC*	
other	/ʌ/		/a/	*ada*
girl	/ɜ:/		/a/	*gyal*
there	/ɛə/		/ɛ/	*de*
the	/ə/, /i:/		/i/	*di*
you	/u:/		/u/	*yu*

One of the striking differences between JC and British dialects of English is that all the short vowels can occur at the end of a word, as happens in four of the five example words above. The word *reggae* is a prime example, though with its general adoption has come the (white) pronunciation 'regay'.

Another striking difference is the amount of nasalization in JC. When /m/ or /n/ follow a vowel they often disappear in rapid or relaxed speech in JC, leaving the preceding vowel nasalized – that is, partly pronounced through the nose.

[2] Such words rhyme in Southern varieties of Black American too. Witness for instance the rhyme in 'Sixteen tons' (the song made famous by Tennessee Ernie Ford):

> Peter don't you call me, 'cause I just can't go
> I owe my soul to the company sto[re].

FIGURE 4.1 *Sound changes between Standard British English and Jamaican Creole**

Standard British English	Jamaican Creole	
	BFY spelling	*Dictionary spelling*
man /a/	/a/ man, pap	-a-
dog, pop /ɒ/		
start /a:/	/a:/ daag, start, all	-aa-
four, all /ɔ:/		
	/uə/ four, show	-uo-
go, show /əu/		
turn /ɜ:/	/ɔ̈/ goh, tu'n, fun	-o-
fun /ʌ/		
bed /ɛ/	/ɛ/ bed, teck	-e-
take, Jamaican /ei/		
wear /ɛə/	/iə/ Jamaican, wear, fear	-ie-
fear /iə/		
boy /ɔi/	/ai/ bwoy/bwai/, like	-ai-
like /ai/		
bounce, shout /au/	/ɔu/ †bounce, shout	-ou-

* /a/ As in Yorkshire or Geordie 'man'.
/a:/ The same sound, twice as long (or more).
/uə/ Similar to SBE 'brewer' or Geordie 'boat'.
/ɔ̈/ Similar to SBE 'hut', but pronounced with slightly rounded lips; the vowel in Geordie 'burn'.
/iə/ Similar to SBE 'pier' or 'ski-er' (one who skis).
/ɔu/ As general American 'so', the **oal** in Cockney 'coal' – JC 'cow' and Cockney 'coal' are pronounced almost identically.
† Standard words ending in /-aun/ often become /-ɔ̃ŋ/ or /-ɔ̃ū/ in JC, so **bounce** is often *bongs* /bɔ̃ŋs/, or /bɔ̃ūs/; **down** is often *dong* /dɔ̃ŋ/, or /dɔ̃ū/, and so on.

Kyaan (can't) is always said *kyāā*, which rhymes, almost, with French *vin*. This is where Black pupils have an advantage over white in learning to pronounce French.

Consonants

The following consonantal sounds in JC are pronounced as in English:

> b, t, d, f, g, j, p, r, s, t, v, w, y, z, sh, ch

(In the phonemic spelling set in italics in this book, the /g/ is as in gift, /j/ as in jest, /r/ following a vowel as in Irish 'cork'.)

/h/ is pronounced more or less as in English in Western Jamaica, but in Central and Eastern parts of the island, including Kingston, it is placed (optionally) before any vowel beginning a word, so that you find:

> *hinglish* alongside *inglish* for **English**
> *hafis* alongside *afis* for **office**

London Jamaican and Bedfordian Jamaican have not opted clearly for either system. Using /h/ as in English (that is, phonemically to distinguish one word from another) is probably more usual, but the 'Hinglish' type of pronunciation has the advantage of sounding especially Jamaican and is also used. /l/ is often 'clear', even at the end of a word, so that in Jamaica pronunciation the /l/ in **sell** is often identical to that in **sell out**. /r/ can be pronounced after vowels. In London and most parts of South Eastern England /r/ has not been pronounced postvocalically since the end of the eighteenth century. Probably it never has been pronounced in JC – until recently. Now it frequently is, where the spelling shows it, after /o/ *skort* (skirt), /uo/ *fuor* (four) and /ie/ *bier* (beer or bear). Educated Jamaicans seem to have introduced this feature, but British Black speakers associate this not with an educated style so much as a Jamaican one, and frequently adopt it themselves. The tendency for nasal consonants /m/ and /n/ occurring after vowels to disappear has already been noted.

Combinations of consonants

Many combinations of consonants that occur in English do not occur in JC or seem recent and only partially accepted introductions. So there is *trang* and *tep* alongside *strang* (strong) and *step*. This is particularly true at the end of a

word where the following clusters do not occur:
/-sk/, /-ld/, /-nd/, /-sp/, /-st/, /-kst/, /-nst/, and all con...
caused by the past tense endings /-t/ and /-ed/ exc...
/-nt/ and /-lt/ which can occur. These combinat...
simplified by dropping the final consonant. Thus in...
For You we find such forms as **groun'**, **stan'-up**, **lif-up**, **jus'**
and so on. However, /z, s/ can follow any consonant that it is
possible for them to follow in English. So English -/sk/ is
frequently -/ks/ in JC: **desk** and **ask** become *deks* and *aks*,
which of course also conforms to a pattern common in
British English dialects.

The consonant combinations /-dl-/ and /-tl-/ in English
words like **middle** and **kettle** become /-gl-/ and /-kl-/ in
Jamaican. So that the nursery rhyme becomes:

> Hey diggle diggle,
> Di kyat an di figgle.

'Jamaican' consonant clusters: /ky/ and /gy/, /pw/ and /bw/
Cassidy's comments (1961) on these Jamaican sounds are
clear and to the point. He shows that the collapsing of four
SBE vowels into two JC ones /a/ and /aa/ does not always
result in 'homophones' (sound-alike pairs of words) by
offering the following comparisons:

BE	Jamaican Folk
cot, cat	/kat, kyat/
corn, can't	/kaan, kyaan/
got, gat	/gat, gyat/
Gordon, garden	/gaadn, gyaadn/

He continues 'If **cot** and **cat** behaved like **pot** and **pat** they
would become complete homonyms, and so would **got** and
gat. But these consonants **k** and **g**, when they precede Standard **a** become **ky** and **gy** in Jamaican, and so a distinction is
still preserved from the words with Standard **o** . . . '. Then
there are the words where SBE /ai/ and /ɔi/ are collapsed into
JC /ai/:

BE	Jamaican Folk
bile, boil	/bail, bwail/
pile, spoil	/pail, pwail/

·Here **p** and **b**, when they precede Standard **oi** become **pw** and **bw** in Jamaican; and so, though the Standard diphthong is lost, a distinction is preserved and homonymy is avoided (Cassidy 1961: 35).

/ny/ is one palatal consonant that is partially of African origin, occurring in words like *nyam* (eat) and *nyaka-nyaka* (slovenly, untidy) (Twi: **nyănkănyănkă**, 'cut into pieces'). *Ballad For You* spells 'boy' **bwoy** and *Park Bench Blues* has **nyam**, which is an archetype of Jamaican Creole, but otherwise the spelling does not indicate these pronunciations (which are very common: *gyal*, for instance, is the normal pronunciation rather than *gal* for 'girl').

Stress and tone

English is a heavily stressed language. JC, like French, is very lightly stressed – compare JC *Jumiekan* with SBE 'Jamaican'. Because of this even spacing of syllables, speakers of JC are possibly more conscious of the difference between long and short vowels than their English counterparts (Jennifer Johnson's spelling often indicates length, for instance). The following words are distinguished very largely by length of vowel – quite simply the long vowels are to be pronounced so that they last twice as long (at least) as the short vowels:

SBE	JC
one	*wan*
want	*waan*
cat	*kyat*
cart	*kyaat*
arm (including the hand)	*han*
horn	*haan*

The difference in length would be well illustrated by asking a Jamaican or Black British friend to pronounce:

wa yu waan?
(What do you want?)

Alright, Granny, which one you want? [lines 180–1]
aarait Grani wichwan yu waan?

Syllables that take the stress in SBE are frequently said with a relatively high pitch in JC. This conveys the impression of stress to English ears: **bu**tter in SBE, *bótà* in JC. At the same time the even-timed flow of syllables makes all Creoles seem strange or difficult to understand to the outsider. The system of pitches instead of stresses is a carry-over from the tonal systems of African languages. At this stage it is not clear whether JC is in fact a tonal language in the sense that Yoruba, Twi or Ibo are, where tone-marking actually enters into the grammatical system. (Two Atlantic Creoles have been recognized as tone languages in this sense: Saramaccan and Ndjuka of Surinam. So has West African Pidgin English.) However, it is becoming clear that Jamaican and other Atlantic Creoles do distinguish between different words on the basis of pitch, even when a distinction is not made (by different stressing) in English. A Barbadian poet Bruce St John stated in a recent broadcast that in Bajan whereas **wórkèr** meant 'one who works', **wòrkér** (with an un-English pattern of pitches – that is, with low pitch on the first syllable, high on the second) meant 'seamstress'. In that case the pitch difference suggests a tone difference in the linguistic sense. Some other words or phrases that were thought to be identical in JC may be distinguished by such tone-marking:

Míerì bróùn		Mièrí Bróùn	
	Mary is brown		Mary Brown
			(example from Lawton 1968)
à fáìt	it's a fight	*á fàìt*	'fighting'
			(continuous form of verb)
kyàn	can	*kyá(a)n*	can't

Naturally there has to be some way of signalling the difference between positive and negative; when *kyá(a)n* means 'can't' the following verb takes a low pitch or tone.

Words of African origin are a different matter again. Here there is no question of high- and low-pitched syllables representing the stresses of an accented language. This is an area of inquiry that should provide a rich field for future research. Intonation is an allied subject of course. In Jamaican a rising intonation alone marks yes/no questions, and indeed, some other constructions are distinguished just by intonation. Thus:

Noh di vicar! [*BFY*, line 107]

would have a level high intonation pattern,

Nóh dí vícár! (In terms of pitch: Noh_4 di_4 vi_4car_4!)

meaning 'The vicar (himself)'. Whereas 'Noh di vicar', with no exclamation mark and a falling intonation pattern, would mean simply 'not the vicar'.

Obviously no pitch, tone or intonation shows up in the printed text of *BFY*. To appreciate not only the pronunciation but the whole impact of the piece white readers are urged to have it read aloud by someone from the British Black community.

CHAPTER 5

A Range of Dialect

THE CONTINUUM: A SPECTRUM OF LANGUAGE

I think I have quite a few dialects and I enjoy using all of them i.e. when I'm angry with a stranger I speak English. At other times when I'm angry with a brother or sister I use a West Indian accent. When I have a play fight with my smaller brother I put on a coarse cockney accent. Ordinarily I have a slight cockney accent. [Marcia, in Richmond 1978]

Why, what do you think the folks say for 'hevn't you?' – the gentry, you know, says 'hevn't you' – well the people about here says 'hanna yey.' It's what they call the dileck as is spoke hereabouts, sir. That's what I've heard Squire Donnithorne say many a time; it's the dileck, says he. [Innkeeper in *Adam Bede*]

Is JC a separate system?

We are all aware that English can be spoken in a range of accents and dialects. We can readily appreciate that geographic separation and perhaps poor communications led originally to the growth of these different varieties. We are also apt to place people we meet on a social or educational scale after hearing them speak just a few words. We can, finally, appreciate the way in which individuals vary their speech to suit the occasion, and that with some people this amounts to switching from one dialect to another. I have already mentioned that JC is arguably a language in its own right but is also joined to standard English by what linguists call a dialect continuum, an unbroken range of dialect with no obvious point at which one variety becomes another.

And of course a continuum of dialect between a local variety and standard (or internationally accepted) English is a commonplace throughout the English-speaking world. A white family in London, for instance, could exhibit a wide range of accent or dialect from the full Cockney of the lorry driver father to the carefully nurtured 'educated' accent his daughter uses during her work as a receptionist. And similarly a family in Kingston, Jamaica, could use a very wide range from JC (or 'Patois') to standard Jamaican English, for the same reasons of job aspirations and social affiliations. Individuals in both families would probably exhibit a range of dialect when speaking together rather than A always speaking variety A and B always speaking variety B. Here the similarity ends. There are two important respects in which the Creole continuum differs from ranges of dialect elsewhere. First there is the sheer distance between the two 'polar' varieties. From the simple standpoint of intelligibility, JC is further away from SE than even the most non-standard Scottish dialects – possibly a fair comparison here would be between Swiss German varieties and standard German, or Catalan and Castilian Spanish. And of course the underlying grammar of JC marks it out as fundamentally different from all non-Creole dialects of English. I would argue that on this level JC differs from SE in the way that a foreign language does. Second, while dialect choice in Jamaica may correlate quite well with social class, in Black Britain this is much less obvious. The complexities of dialect selection in a Black British community will be discussed in detail in the next chapter, but let me say concisely at this point that the real motivation for selecting one dialect or the other has relatively little to do with the English class system as such and a great deal to do with ethnic and cultural identification.

These two differences can be captured by one generalization: Jamaican Creole is a language caught up with English in a dialect continuum. This helps to explain the wayward fashion in which different continuum varieties are very commonly used together by many Black British speakers. Consider the following:

An' so Brother **Haansi** and the girl, they went a-rolling, rolling down into the sea. And a crab came **an bite Broda Haansi pan im leg. Broda**

Haansi spring up as a light an im rub im leg. And all the lizard come **an bite-off im toe. An di gyal** say, **di gyal seh** that 'I want to marry you honey'. An' so **Broda Haansi** said, 'All right, he can, baby'. [April – 8-year-old girl in Bedford]

Maxine: Where's Audrey, Marcia. I want to lend one of her tapes.
Audrey: **Hey, Diana go easy wid de drinks den. Member seh is only 4 more bottles** we have left.
Diana: You better go and change the records.
Diana: Marcia do you know where I've mislaided my Christmas pudden.
Marcia: **Listen man don't worry bout Christmas pudden.**[1] **You nah go dead if you no have none.**
Diana: **Awright man.**
Maxine: **Who dat bwoy over dear ah-whine-in himself. Mussi tink him a something big.**

[Jamaican Story]

The second example, from the script of a play written by senior pupils at Vauxhall Manor School, London, is particularly interesting. The switches between 'lects' have nothing to do with confusion or woolly-mindedness. Audrey's stage directions throughout the play (Audrey was the scribe) are in unerring standard English, impeccably spelt. Rather than diminishing the status of JC as a stable language, separable from English, it could be argued that such rapid switching actually confirms it. Clearly there are two very different varieties here to mix and intersperse. Such linguistic behaviour is in fact common in bilinguals *when speaking amongst themselves*. Just compare the rapid switching between Spanish and English of this bilingual in an 'in-group' conversation:

Mm-huh, Yeah, An' ... an' they tell me, 'How did you quit, Mary?' I di'n' quit, I ... I just stopped. I mean it wasn' an effort I made **que voy a dejar de fumar porque me hace dano o** [that I'm going to stop smoking because its harmful to me, or ...] this or that, uh-uh. It just ... that ... eh ... I used to pull butts out of the ... the ... the waste paper basket. Yeah [Laughter]. I used to go look in the [unclear]. **Se me acababan los cigarros en la noche** [my cigarettes would run out at night]. [Gumperz and Hernandez-Chavez 1972 : 97]

[1] This line could be taken as quite broad Creole, or not, depending on pronunciation.

It is almost certainly true that JC is a separate or at least separable language from English, as an abstract system, as a psychological reality to its speakers, and even as an actual spoken variety. Yet this 'position' is surprisingly controversial, and indeed difficult to defend. Not only do laymen find it hard to conceive of Creoles as anything but 'mish-mashes', linguists have found it challenging to come to terms with the systematicity that lies behind their highly variable nature.

The problem is that nearly all Jamaican language in Jamaica, as well as in Britain, is neither (extreme) Creole nor English but falls in between, 'on the continuum'. Does this mean, to put it bluntly, that 'real' Creole hardly exists, that the rules of JC grammar that we looked at in chapter 4 are in fact never consistently used but constantly subject to interference from the rules of English? V. Edwards (1979b), in a discussion on phonology along the continuum, argues convincingly that for her informant at least 'there are not two mutually exclusive systems' (English and Creole). I would argue that the systems are not normally exclusive and that the speaker in question, Angella, does not use them exclusively, but that there *are* two systems. If the JC continuum has been brought about by interference (the interacting of two varieties, two sets of grammars), as is generally accepted, what is interfering with what? Is English, which clearly exists as a separate system, interfering with Creole, which does not? Or, in the case of Angella, does her 'English', something which is neither English nor Creole, interfere with her 'Creole', something which is also neither English nor Creole? Obviously this is a highly complex question. The linguist Labov as usual goes to the heart of the matter:

The problem for Creole is in locating a well-defined set of norms at the Vernacular end – to demonstrate that the language *actually used* is more than a set of deviations from Standard. [Labov 1972: 454; my emphases]

In a sense we have already demonstrated this, informally. *Ballad For You* (and speech at the same point on the continuum) seems to have its own grammatical integrity, quite different from English, in the rules for copula use and so on that I have examined. There are respects in which *BFY* language is not really 'end-of-continuum'. First there are relatively superficial differences from the recognized extreme, such as the use of **shi** and **har** for **im** feminine. Second, in addition to all the Creole features, there are a few intrusions from more English varieties, such as **There is a common room** and **Dem was fightin** instead of **One common room dey deh** and **Dem did a fight**.

Beryl Loftman Bailey provided an answer to Labov's challenge–before he issued it in fact–when she published *Jamaican Creole Syntax* (1966). Bailey, a Jamaican herself who grew up speaking both the Patois and standard English, brought to the subject not only her expertise as a linguist but also her intuitions as a native speaker. In her introduction she dealt briefly with the variation that I have been discussing, and described how a speaker might shift back and forth from Creole to English without even being conscious of the shift. She observed that most investigators of language in Jamaica have encountered 'extreme difficulty in distinguishing between the various layers of the language structure' (Bailey 1966: 1). The image of layers of onion skin with broad Creole at the heart is a refreshing change from the usual linear model of a continuum that, oddly, comes to an end with nothing beyond it. She then proceeded to describe Jamaican Creole, which is one of the two systems that causes the variation. Implicit in her book is that JC is a reality. It generates all the other varieties through direct or indirect interaction with English.

Jamaican Creole Syntax is still the definitive work on the language. However, it did not seem to resolve the problem of Creole variation to the satisfaction of other linguists. Bailey (1966) is not of course a study of the variation within JC. It is plain, however, that she saw this work as providing a starting point from which the variation could be studied. The theory of dialect mixture, which Bailey is in effect putting forward, was not a popular linguistic theory in the sixties and seventies. Also it has generally been assumed that the variety that she describes is a construct rather than a real living language. But Bailey seems to envisage her extreme variety of Jamaican Creole both as a construct, a factor in the interaction – JC x English = continuum varieties – and as an actual speech variety. The latter is inescapable, since most of the very large number of examples of 'Baileyan' JC scattered throughout the book are things that Jamaicans have actually said. However, Bailey has made a selection from the speech data she collected. She explains that she distinguished between extreme Creole and other varieties on the basis of her native speaker intuitions, or 'sprachgefühl' as she puts it. She also drew on the intuitions of her informants. When these people produced utterances for Bailey that were less than broad Creole they were told (by Bailey's assistant)

> *im no waant it datde wie, a di jagwa taak im waan.*
> (Not like that, it's broad Creole she wants.)

This procedure may not sound very scientific. And yet it may be valid in the last analysis. It is obviously very important to tap the native speaker insights of the community; all that is lacking here, perhaps, is a method of cross-checking the validity of the results.

Another unexpected aspect of Bailey's work is that she takes as given that there is but one extreme variety to be described, subject to quite minor geographic variation within Jamaica. This is surprising since Jamaica is 145 miles long and has a great deal of mountainous terrain, separating originally isolated areas, where one would expect different dialects to grow up. In an appendix, Bailey lists a small number of geographic variants, such as **de** for **a** in Western parishes. She also lists a small number of JC variant features as 'English' – that is, borrowings from English that regularly occur in even the broadest speakers' output, in broadest style. She includes **woz** + verb + **in** as in **dem was fightin'** in this latter category.

Later, Bailey published a paper entitled *Can Dialect Boundaries be Defined?* (1971) which takes the theme of dialect mixture one stage further. In this paper she describes a method by which all Jamaican language can be placed on the continuum. In this, the number of systematic changes that have to be made to translate a text into standard are scored, and then those necessary for translation into Creole are also scored. When the scores are placed side by side they are said to give a ratio of creoleness to standardness. The scores, however, are complex, with any change in sentence type scoring 5, and other changes scoring less, down to lexical and phonological changes both scoring only 1. She maintains that there is, ultimately, a divide between JC and SE. Whereas some features – such as the phonology – vary smoothly between the two extremes, there are other features, such as types of sentence structure, that basically belong to either JC or SE and that mark language as belonging to one side or the other.

Variation across the continuum

In the Bedford Survey on the speech of Black children in the locality, an attempt was made to create a model of the continuum using a modification of Bailey's method. Briefly, 32 texts were selected from a pool of recordings and these were then transcribed in phonetic script. They were chosen on the basis of homogeneity – that is, they showed no obvious large-scale internal switches of dialect – and also on the basis of the range that it was hoped to illustrate, from broad JC to 'broad' English. (For a full account of the Phonological Continuum Model (PCM) and the complete 32 texts, see Sutcliffe 1978.) Clearly it would have been better to have had a larger number of transcripts, but the operation was limited by time. These transcribed passages were then ordered according to the creoleness of their sound system by placing them on the phonological continuum between the two extreme varieties. To do this, a scoring system derived from Bailey was used. This meant that any passage (and they varied in length between 100 and 300 words) that had only South Eastern English vowel sounds in it scored 0, and any passage that used only the Baileyan inventory of JC vowel sounds, correctly distributed, of course, scored 100. Passages in between the two achieved a rating between 0 and 100, depending on their interspersing and blending of the two sound systems.[2] The results were quite pleasing. The scoring enabled the 32 passages to be ranged in order of creoleness

[2] Compare the very similar methodology developed by Silverman to study the phonology of Puerto Rican and Black speakers in New York (1975).

across the complete spectrum – one passage scored 100 per cent and the most English passage scored 4 per cent. Only two or three passages seemed out of order, and these were cases where the grammar of the piece was noticeably more Creole than the phonology or vice versa. In general, the levels of grammar and the sound system varied along the continuum seemingly in step with each other, giving some kind of insight into how these changes were modulated and orchestrated. Afterwards, various features of the grammar in the passages were given special attention. The use of the copula (verb **to be** equivalent), the marking of simple past tense (walked, came, etc.) and the incidence of Creole personal pronouns (*mi, im,* etc.) were all scored for the complete range of passages.

Let us look at the scores for the copula, as this is something that will again bring the problem of variation into focus. The averaged scores for the texts, rather arbitrarily divided into three groups roughly representing a third of the continuum each, are shown in figure 5.1. There are (obviously) more passages in the 1–13 and 21–32 groups, due simply to clustering of the results in these thirds. The bar graphs represent the percentage of the respective copulas appearing in the texts before noun phrases, progressive verbs (past and present) and adjectives. Thus if there were four cases where pre-adjectival copulas might have been used in a group of passages, and in one case **be** was used: *im iz blak,* and in the others ϕ (zero morpheme, i.e. no copula is used): *im blak,* then the **be** score would be 25 per cent. This is simply a method of showing how the grammar is operating at a particular point on the continuum.

Scores for locative copula (*de* in Creole: *im **de** iina di kichin*) are not shown, because very few opportunities for it occurred in the PCM passages, and as a result scores are uncharacteristic. The other scores are very much as one would expect. The particle *a* is a broad Creole form and so only occurs in the Creole third – before progressive verbs (*im **a** waak huom*) and noun phrases (*im **a** mi faada*). Noun phrases also never occur with zero copula, at least in these passages. It is a rule in JC, as I have noted, that the copula before such noun phrases is always *a* or *iz*.

What is not clear-cut here is the pattern of copula use before adjectives. The 'rule' is that predicate adjectives do not need a copula (*im big, shi tuu fiesti*), and yet even in the most Creole third of the texts, 40 per cent of the adjectives are breaking this rule and being introduced by a form of the verb **to be** (*iz, woz*) – it is almost as if the rule is dis-

FIGURE 5.1 *Copula use in the Phonological Continuum Model passages (Bedford Survey). The bargraphs show proportions*

(a)   Creole copula use (PCM passages 1–13)

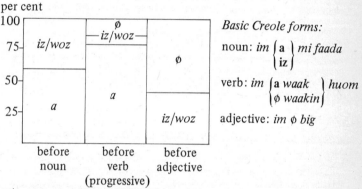

Basic Creole forms:

noun: *im* {*a* / *iz*} *mi faada*

verb: *im* {*a waak* / *ϕ waakin*} *huom*

adjective: *im ϕ big*

iz/woz can be considered typical Creole copulas although they are almost identical in sound to English forms **is** and **was**.

(b)   Mid-continuum copula use (PCM passages 14–20)

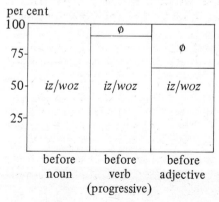

(c)   English copula use (PCM passages 21–32)

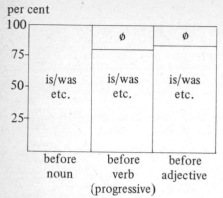

English forms:

noun: he **is/was** my father

verb: he is **is/was** walking

adjective: he **is/was** big

φ zero morpheme

integrating. Yet the native speaker intuition of Bailey – and others – has been that (predicate) adjectives are a sort of verb and do not need copulas.

The copula scores for Jennifer Johnson's *Ballad For You* and its companion piece *Park Bench Blues* are very revealing on this. Here the rules are more consistently applied than in the PCM passages. There are two explanations for this. In the first place the PCM texts score is an averaged one – it includes slightly less than broad Creole texts along with the really broad, and within the texts of course the same kind of variation. Secondly, and this is really the same point, Bailey and other native speakers can see a pattern beyond the variation. Jennifer Johnson, for instance, in writing *BFY* consciously in broad JC (I repeat, not for the purposes of this book) *may* be idealizing the rules. She may be, as it were, sifting the Creole grammar from the rest, though not in any over-deliberate artificial way. This is not a *linguist's* construct, and indeed not really a construct at all, since it is a creative piece of actual (written) language use. Her scores for copula use are shown in figure 5.2. (The language of the two mothers in these stories was not scored together with the narrator and the girls because their JC is superficially different – they use more *a* copulas before noun phrases, for instance.) *Woz* can be usefully considered as a past tense marker, rather than a

FIGURE 5.2 *Copula use in* Ballad For You *and* Park Bench Blues
        (narrator and girls)

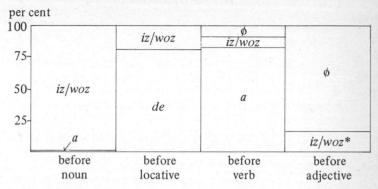

* *iz* once, *woz* twice
φ zero morpheme

copula, when it appears before Creole verbs and adjectives.
As such it is a variant of Creole *ben* and *did*. If you take out
the two *woz* tokens from the narrator/girls' pre-adjectival
score there is only the one occurrence of *iz* and the zero
copula score becomes 94 per cent. In other words the Creole
copula rules are now scarcely broken at all. It is worth noting
that in this and other major respects the grammars of Beryl
Bailey and Jennifer Johnson are in agreement with those of
the ultimately broad Sranan Creole. In fact, even speakers of
Black American vernacular, where one might have suspected
a saturation effect from standard English, tend to keep to
these copula rules – and some Black teenagers recorded in
New York City by William Labov were found to adhere to
them almost completely! (cf. Baugh, n.d., and his reanalysis
of speech data from the Cobras). Baugh comments: ' . . . the
quantitative confirmation which emerges from the present
analysis establishes the Creole ancestry of contemporary BEV
[Black English vernacular] beyond any doubt'.
   One final piece of support for Beryl Bailey's thesis comes
from the most Creole of the 32 PCM texts (with a virtually
100 per cent Creole phonology rating). This was a story told
by a 16-year-old Jamaican boy Michael at school in Luton.
The circumstances in which he told it are interesting in them-

selves. He told it directly to me in a one-to-one interview, and it is a truism in sociolinguistics that such situations tend to produce formal speech (which in all normal circumstances means a shift towards standard). However, he had been played a taped sentence:

Mi naa tekaaf no Ko:t, a mai Ko:t so mi a kiip it aan.

This was a recording of a British-born Black girl, plainly talking JC but not quite the JC extreme. When asked if this was 'Jamaican' (i.e. JC) he replied that it was, but not as Jamaican as he sometimes talked when socializing with friends of his own age. By way of illustration he told this story about Big Head, Big Belly and Kenge Foot. It is in paradigmatic Baileyan JC except for the two features that Michael himself edits out – and *woz* at least is a feature that Bailey lists as an English intrusion, common in broad JC.

Tri breda **went** *a dakta, go a dakta . . . an di dakta tel dem se . . . wel wan a dem* **woz** *. . . dem a big ed, di ada wan a big beli an di ada wan a kenge fut. So dakta tel big ed se ef im shiek im hed im hed wi drap aaf . . . dakta tel big beli se him laaf him beli wi bos. an im tel kenge fut se ef im ron, graastraa wi kot aaf im fut . . . so neks die big ed go klaim apl tri an en nyam di apl-dem an mm . . . big beli aas im fi . . . apl an big ed shiek im ed an se 'no', an im hed drap aaf . . . an big beli sit . . . stanop doun de a laaf an im beli bos, an kenge fut a ron go tel dakta an graastraa kotaaf im fut.*

(Three brothers went to the doctor and the doctor told them that . . . well one of them was Big Head, the other one was Big Belly and the other one was Kenge (puny) Legs. So the doctor told Big Head that if he shook his head his head would fall off, and he told Big Belly that if he laughed, his belly would burst, and he told Kenge Legs that if he ran the grass would cut his legs off. So next day Big Head went and climbed an apple tree and ate the apples. Big Belly came down with Kenge Foot, and Big Belly asked him for an apple. Big Head shook his head and said 'no' and his head fell off. And Big Belly stood down there laughing and his belly burst. And Kenge Legs was running to tell the doctor and the grass cut his legs off.)

For an Akan parallel to this tale, see 'Ashanti Story', a poem by Efua Morgue (in Bassir 1957) in which the three brothers, sons of Anansi himself, are called Waddle (Big Belly), Thud

(Big Head) and Spindly (Kenge Foot). A Trinidadian version of this tale is featured in the Texts at the end of the book.

Individual ranges

Something should be said about the dialect ranges along the continuum of those speakers I recorded for the Bedford Survey, and especially those whose texts form the PCM. In general, the ranges exhibited were wider than the literature suggests for Caribbean areas, and this is not really surprising. Black British children have a full exposure to standard and other completely uncreolized dialects of English, and they socialize with children from many ethnic backgrounds. On the other hand there is more and more pressure on them, as they grow up, to establish an 'Afro' identity and improve their grasp of broad JC. In some cases speakers produced a span of dialect that stretched almost from one end of the continuum to the other. Michael, whom I have quoted above, was one such. A year after providing the ultimately broad *Tri Breda* text he gave an impromptu talk on Rastafarianism to a group of sceptical Black youths. Just before he started he was asked whether he wanted to give the talk in 'Jamaican'. He replied that he would be using English:

The RasTafari faith is based on the teachings of Marcus Garvey. He's a Jamaican Pan-Africanist who was born in nineteen sixteen and he teached about ... He was a profit and a visionary and ... he told the Black people that in nineteen thirty there would be a Black King born [*sic*] in Africa, and the Black people should look unto him for refuge. And he preached all over America and in Jamaica. And when he was in America he upset the Government so they expelled him from the Country. And he went back to Jamaica and he preached as well so he was expelled. They told him to ... *waantid* him to leave the Country ...

Here Michael's language is undeniably English. The phonology is that of standard Jamaican English with one intrusive Creole pronunciation: **waantid** for 'wanted'. The range this represents is, of course, enormous for a dialect speaker, and easily construable as bilingualism, although Michael also speaks intervening varieties on the continuum. Full exemplification of a British-born speaker with an equally wide range is given later in this chapter, where five different PCM texts from Patricia illustrate five shifts along the dialect spectrum.

Dialect boundaries

Bailey's concept of a dialect boundary between JC and SE runs counter both to the concept of a continuum and to linguists' recent thinking on dialect variation. As Peter Trudgill puts it:

In the case of both regional and social variation it has to be pointed out that it is hardly ever possible to draw a clear dividing line between one dialect or accent and another. Dialects and accents are not discrete or separate entities. [Trudgill 1975: 22]

This generalization applies in any number of cases throughout the English language area and elsewhere too. One would have thought that it applied even more so, if anything, to the Jamaican Creole continuum. It is known as the continuum because that is what it is: 'an unbroken mass or tissue or course of matter, sensation, events etc.' (*Concise Oxford Dictionary*). And yet there *is* a dialect boundary on the range of PCM passages. More evidence is needed before such a controversial finding is taken as widely applicable – but the evidence we have is unequivocal. What happens is that certain very obviously Creole grammatical features suddenly cut out about a quarter of the way along the continuum from the JC extreme. This is particularly clear-cut in the case of two sets of features that occur very commonly: the progressive (or continuative) verb markers *a* and *de*, and the set of JC personal pronouns (*mi, yu, im, wi, unu, dem, fi-mi*, etc.). The pattern emerges clearly in table 5.1, in which PCM passage 1 is most Creole and 17 much less Creole in terms of phonology. The column headed 'JC specified' indicates whether or not speaker or researcher actually said that the language was to be 'Jamaican' or 'Patois'. The continuative marker *a* (etc.) occurs frequently in all passages 1–11 except in 5 where there are no opportunities for it to occur. Then it drops out suddenly and completely. At almost the same point, the high level of JC pronouns drops to a very low level or nil. The one passage that ruffles this pattern, 14, is aberrant in other ways. Although the speaker in this passage, Peggy, a 14-year-old girl from Jamaica, specifies JC, she varies her language from ***an im se tu i waif no fi toch i*** to **an' he went back into the woods**. Every other speaker in the PCM

TABLE 5.1 *PCM passages 1–17 showing the cut-off point for JC*

	PCM passage	Continuative marker	JC pronouns	JC phonology (per cent)	JC specified
Michael	1	+	+	99.5	+
Patricia	2	+	+	95.3	–
	3	+	+	95.1	+
	4	+	+	93.3	+
	5	(no sites)	+	90.7	+
	6	+	+	85.4	+
	7	+	+	85.2	+
	8	+	+	82.4	+
	9	+	?*	82.2	–
	10	+	+	81.2	+
	11	+	+	78.4	+
Patricia	12	–	+	74.7	–
	13	(no sites)	–	73.0	+
Peggy	14	–	+	65.8	+
	15	–	–	58.8	–
	16	–	–	58.6	–
Patricia	17	–	–	48.4	–

* The '?' for the pronoun realizations for passage 9 indicates that JC pronouns occurred, but at a lower frequency (35%) – whereas the '+' for passages 1–12 and 14 indicates a high frequency, generally 75 per cent or more, with the main intrusions of 'English' pronouns being **shi**, **har** and **it**.

who deliberately switched into Creole switched into the zone of high realization of JC pronouns and continuative particles represented by passages 1–11.

Some other important aspects of the grammar such as past tense marking do not show sudden cut-off points, but evolve towards English along the continuum. It is important to note that the two features I have looked at that suddenly cut out are relatively superficial. For example, the Creole progressive non-past verb behaves much the same in the mid-continuum texts as in the 'JC quarter' texts; it is just 'spelt' or realized as *singin* (etc.) in the former and *a sing* (and sometimes *singin*) in the latter. Superficial though these features are, they contribute strongly to the 'feel' or impact of the language. It seems likely that they act as markers of JC in the same way as **ain't** and double negatives act as obvious markers of non-standard speech in other communities. We need more evidence, but on the strength of what we have so far it would appear that the community has a common concept of what is and what is not 'Jamaican' or 'Patois' and where it ends on the continuum. There is also a suggestion that some speakers, at least, perceive beyond this the ultimate grammar rules, and actual dialect, of extreme Creole described by Bailey. Can dialect boundaries be defined? Perhaps in this special case they can, after all.

AN ILLUSTRATION OF THE BRITISH JAMAICAN CONTINUUM (BEDFORD)

Patricia, a British-born Black girl aged 13 in 1974, was one of a group of girls attending Parkwood School, Bedford, who were recorded over periods totalling more than five hours. Patricia probably contributed most. Five 'pieces' by her, in focused dialects from English through various intermediate stages to broad Jamaican Creole, are printed here. Together, the five texts (which appear in the Phonological Continuum Model) illustrate a very wide range indeed. However, most of her speech was not focused on one dialect in this way (at least when talking informally in a peer group atmosphere). A narrative that is not confined to any one point on the continuum, but ranges widely, is included after the five texts.

(1) *A conversation with her mother at home (mother's words omitted)*

Tons of the children didn't have any coats (...) yeah (...) no, was a different girl ... She got knocked off her bike (...) I think she did 'cos she wou'nt be comin' down Gladstone Street (...) a thought she (...) poor thing ... hey, she said she's ... Mr. K. said she's lying in hospital ... lying in hospital very, very ... (...) she **was** unconscious when I saw her (...) yeah she was (...) she was just like that other man (...) a don't know ... she just said ... said she's lying in hospital (...) her bicycle had her name (...) carve her name on bikes (...) a no thought she woulda carved her name on her bike. [PCM text 32]

(2) *Retelling the story of a horror film*

This woman she was in her bed ... the husband had died ... it was the husband that was mm ... doin' all the killin' ... he had died long time ago and he had 'is Egyptian ring on (...) a curse was on i dat who die wi' this ring will live again, and the only way you can break that curse is to take the ring off ... well mm ... di girl hear this man bang ... you know crash of glass ... she go outside into [th]is summerhouse and take di gun ... and after the husband 'd died she never gone in there again ... so ... and no window was broken (...) di door ... di lock was forced ... not wid any kin' a weapon ... it was just like it was turned or some'ing like that ... well she went in there wi' di gun an di dog an a torch ... [PCM text 23]

(3) *Narrative*

Say 'Oh, can I help?' And I took off the record. I want to do every- thing that was there; everything seem excitin'. And er ... the man ax for some ... mm ... a pint o' beer. I took the half glass. I fill i. I give it to im, and 'e give me 'i right ... 'e don[t] even notice yet. 'E give me di right money. A put it in, and after 'e se: 'C'n ave another pint?' Gi me right money again an I still give him, you know, wid di half, half a pint cup, mug. And 'e don[t] even notice. And after 'e said, im se: 'Goo'bye now'. An' a see a child, you know. And after I sell the other man, an he wanted a half, an I give him a pint, pint cup. [PCM text 17]

(4) *Retelling the story of a horror film*

... try to open dis box and 'i white boy cut imsel' ... den after sud- denly di boy was (...) bandage an doin' it up fi 'im an suddenly dis ting dis op ... 'im dis go so like ... im open i ... dis kin' a box ... coffin an ma ... 'im close ... 'e mouth was close den an 'im ... 'im stan'up so an get out di grave ... I mean 'i coffin, an den after 'e open 'e mout' an 'e walkin down like 'at ... an go-in aaah! showin' 'e teet' ... an di blood dis drippin' down di mout in it? (...) an 'en after 'e jus' take di bwoy han' an jus' gone suck out di blood. [PCM text 12, modified standard orthography]

In modified *Dictionary of Jamaican English* orthography (4) would read:

... trai tu opin dis baks an i wait boi kot imsel ... den aafta sodenli di bai woz (...) bandij an duin it ʌp fi im an sodinli dis ting dis o:p ... 'im dis go so laik ... im o:pin i ... dis kaina baks ... kafin an ma ... im klo:z ... i mauf woz klo:z den an im ... im stanop so an get out di griev ... ai miin i kaafin an den aafta i o:pin i mout an i waakin down

laik at an go-in a:::, sho:-in i tiit . . . an di blod dis dripin doun di mout init? (. . .) an en aafta i jis tek di bwai han an dis gaan (. . .) sok out di blod.

(5) *Narrative about the family*

Las' time mi daddy an mi mummy come in mi bedroom an shi seh . . . an' daddy seh 'gi mi a kiss' . . . mi seh 'no man, mi feel like go a sleep' . . . an mi mumma . . . a seh . . . a seh 'no **dad**', not 'no man' [explaining a slip of the tongue she had just made] . . . an mi mummy seh 'gi mi a kiss' . . . mi seh mi feel (. . .) (. . .) shi wan' bathe me . . . mi come upstairs an mi seh 'oh no mum' . . . mi jus' gone ge' mi ves' an mi' stay up dere 'till i gone (. . .) mi seh 'no can bathe miself!' [PCM text 2, modified standard orthography]

In *Dictionary of Jamaican English* orthography (5) would read:

laas taim mi dadi an mi momi kom im mi bedruum an shi se . . . an dadi se 'gi mi a kis' . . . mi se 'no man, mi fiil laik go a sliip' . . . an mi muma . . . a se . . . a se 'no dad' nat no man! an momi se 'gimi a kis' . . . mi se mi fiil (. . .) (. . .) shi waan bied mi . . . mi kom opstiez an mi se 'o nuo mom' . . . mi dis gaan ge mi ves an mi ste op dier til i gaan (. . .) mi se 'no kan bied miself!'

(The wording of (5) has been altered slightly for reasons of confidentiality, but not in any way that would affect the continuum placing of the piece – one sentence has been omitted, and two other words changed.)

'The Club' – A narrative by Patricia

Patricia: We go visit my uncle an then after . . . mi mumma go to um . . . the shop, and go buy books for me and Claudia [her sister] and nightie. And then after me, and C . . . you know, wi a run [were running] bout di place and wi just tek a batl a Coke and wi drink about six batl a Coke dat day and mi sister just stay up stairs a play wid im dally [her dolly]. And then after mi go a stairs an mi see de . . . I see this machine you punch 5 pence in it, and if it 'tick, tick, tick' you win some money. But the other one 'as to be 'tick, tack, toe' before you get the jackpot. And, I said mm . . . 'I never win the jackpot, I don't even know what it is.' So I jus put mi 5 pence in it, all I see's just 'wam' 5 pence, jes kalap over the floor! I got the jackpot and then after I pick it up and I put it in mi bag. And

I have to take up mi every-ting that was in mi bag, and mi Bible that I carry with me, cos I forgot to put it, put it on mi dressin' table. And den after mi see dis men gamblin'. You turn this thing – you 'ave to – is a tiny little thing and you turn it, and whatever you land on like say 'take all' or ... the player after you takes all, or something like that. Or loose it.

Q: You spin the thing?

Moira: Yeah, oh yeah, I know.

Patricia: I said 'Could I 'ave a try?' He say: 'You children shouldn't gamble.' I say: 'Come on let's have a go.' And ... he say 'all right then but don't let a copper come in 'ere.' I say: 'I 'on care about copper.' Even ca ... I call 'em blue bottles. An den after I, we dis [just] spin de thing an I say, and the you know is 50 pence, 50 p an all em ... dere a pound dere. And I put a penny on. Dis a penny and I turn a thing and i said 'take all', every minute, every minute. Mi dis seh, mi seh 'You better go upstairs now, an 'ave a drink Coca-Cola. I'll buy you one'. An so they all, they put it all, you know the other men give him some money to put it on, buy me a tin o coke, and 'ey got on wid di game. I go upstairs an after come back down an seh 'I'm too lonely'. An Claudia seh [imitates little girl voice]: 'Come on, Jenny, let's go an play.' An ... you know, she got this little Dolly. She call it Jenny – stupid idiot [under her breath]. An mm ... I go back downstairs an I play some record. Mi uncle come in an seh: 'You bin causin' trouble again, gamblin'?' 'E said 'Wa's all i about gamblin'? Every time yuh a gamble.' I said 'Is only first time. Anyway look at ... besides look how a money mi gat. So well, mi no know wa yuh qua'l bout.' An 'e se: 'Aa right den a wi get aaf sen'in out di beer ... sellin' di beer.' Say 'Oh, can I help?' And I took off the record. I want to do everything that was there; everything seem excitin'. And er ... the man ax for some ... mm ... a pint o' beer. I took the half glass. I fill i. I give it to im, and 'e give me 'i right ... 'e don[t] even notice yet. 'E give me di right money. A put it in, an after 'e se: 'C'n ave another pint?' Gi me right money again an I still give him, you know, wid di half, half a pint cup, mug. An 'e don[t] even notice. And after 'e said, im se: 'Goo'bye now.' An a see a child, you know. And after I sell the other man, an he wanted a half, an I give him a pint, pint cup. Cos er, when I realise is when dem aal gone. Dat I give them, an they give me um ... either half it or full. So.

Q: They paid double.

Patricia: mm! An some pay less ... because give dem, when dey wanted half a pint. I give them full pint.

Q: So it equals out, in the end.

Patricia: But mm ... Oh God mi mummy come down. She say 'What you doin' 'ere?' An started tellin' me off, an se ... and after she said 'I never know' mmm – she knew the man name. 'I never know 'e started talkin' pint, he usually has halves.' An se, I say 'Is at a pint cup?' And den after she say 'Patricia. A wa yuh do? Di man mos a rab yuh, yuh know.' And mm – she mm – she start cussin me. But when I tell im dat de other man ... after I realise dat dis mus be di mm, half, di half pint one, I say: 'I don' ... he don[t] rob me at all. Cos di oder one must pay me, mm, full, you know, a pint for di half pint.' An – mm – she just burs' out laughing an mi uncle start say 'You mus' come 'ere more often. A wi get more money.'

THE WIDER LINGUISTIC BACKGROUND

How typical is Patricia's language in its various degrees? Her range is comprehensive and her most Creole dialect is plainly a 'full' Jamaican Creole, with a phonology (or pronunciation) only fractionally less broad than the Creole extreme of, for instance, Michael – who told the story of 'The Three Brothers' in Baileyan JC. In fitting Patricia's speech into the total context of Black British speech and white – not something we can do with definitive precision at this point – many questions arise. What follows is an attempt to deal with the most salient.

The English dialect of the Black community in Bedford

Patricia's first passage above was the most English, not only in the Phonological Continuum Model where it scored 4 per cent Creole phonology, but in more than five hours of recordings. Yet it still sounds vaguely Jamaican in terms of rhythm and voice quality, and there is at least one *overtly* Jamaican vowel sound /ɔ̈/ for /ʌ/ in **other**. More striking in a way is the fact that although Patricia came to school from a very decayed area of housing known as the Black Tom, she has no trace of a local white working-class accent. For instance, where the latter has /aɪ/ in **night** (the London sound) or even /ʊɪ/ (suggesting 'noit' or a 'point' of beer), Patricia and other local Black speakers had /ʌɪ/ – that is, the middle-class variant that starts further forward in the mouth. The same discrepancy is found with the /eɪ/ sound in **name**, and again Patricia and other local Blacks produced the 'middle-class' sound. The same again is true, perhaps to a lesser degree, for the full complement of English vowel sounds, except /ʌ/ as in **other**, **tough**, which frequently becomes Jamaican /ɔ/ – almost the **o** of 'hot'. There are several contributory factors to thank here. One is the apparent lack of feeling of solidarity with white working class – at least at the deepest level. However, Patricia and her friends do tend to produce some 'Cockney' sounds, most notably /v/ and /f/ for mo**th**er and **th**in (etc.). This style of pronunciation enables the speaker to avoid producing on the one hand the dental fricatives (too standard, too 'difficult?') and on the other the dental stops /d/ and /t/ (too Creole for English dialect). Such pronunciations also occur in Black American vernacular.

The second most English text in the PCM, from Peter, a British-born boy aged 10 years, scored 8 per cent (Peter also provided the humorous dialogue with Gregory in chapter 2). Peter's text shows the same features: middle-class vowel sounds (except Jamaican /ɔ/ for /ʌ/) and 'Cockney' fricatives. He even shows the same tendency to lisp /s/ + /z/ which seems to be a widespread secondary feature of Black speech. However, the grammar he uses is even more interesting:

Well mm one night before me 'n my bruvver went to bed we had to check that the windows were close' an insteada say ... insteada my bruvver sayin' dat de windows are close' he goes ... 'cos [th]ere's [th]is Bogey Man who we talk about ... an he says 'the windows is very good an Bogey-proof ... and he turned off the light before er, I went ... I got into the bed.' He said 'a Bogey Man is just jumpin' fru de window!' ... an he had [h]is pillow already in [th]e bed ... so I, I just knocked 'im out of the bed and jomped in ... an den he turn on the light 'gain seh 'boy what you doin' there?'

Apart from **the windows is**, which may or may not be an idiosyncracy or a dyed-in-the-wool Cockney feature, there

are at least two grammatical constructions that appear to be
basically Creole but remodelled to fit in with the English.
The remodelling partly consists of anglicizing the pronunciation. Firstly, the JC equivalent of **insteada say** would be
insteda se followed directly by the complement of the clause.
Peter aborts this construction and reverts to the English:
insteada my bruvver sayin' .... Secondly, there is a consecutive verb construction that blends fairly well with the English:
'and den he **turn** on the light 'gain **seh**'. **Seh** here in its Creole
form links with 'turn' without any joining conjunction.
Other consecutive and serial verb constructions would be
instantly recognizable as non-English:

> I was considering weda fi mek Tony **bring** im sound
> **come.** [Greater Mafia in *Wasted Women* 1978]
> (... whether to let Tony bring his sound-system.)

– and so would not appear in 'English'. The final clause in
Peter's text: 'boy what you doin' there?' is ambiguous between an English grammar interpretation: 'Boy what (are)
you doin' there?', and a Creole interpretation in which no
copula (verb **to be**) is missing and one simply has 'boy' +
interrogative word + you + Creole continuous verb + 'there'.
Note that the English interpretation sentence has inversion –
the swapping round of subject and verb – to indicate a question; this verb 'are' – actually just *part* of the verb – is then
elided in rapid, colloquial English. It seems that the English
dialect of Black British speakers plays on such ambiguities.
Other grammatical features that could be noted briefly at
this point as being common to both non-standard English
and Creole:

Non-standard English	*Creole forms*
he don't know	im don't/*duon*/know
he ain't stupid	im ain /ɛ̃/ stupid
ain't it?	ennit? (this British JC form can be used univer- sally – that is, like 'n'est- ce pas' in French)
we was singin'	we *woz* singin.

The above Creole forms are all variants. For instance **im don't**

know is commonly expressed as **im no know** in both JC and British JC. Double negatives and **never** as a past tense negator are also common to both non-standard English and Creole.

British JC in Bedford and elsewhere

It would be useful if we could compare the British Jamaican Creole emerging in London and Bedfordshire (Bedford and Luton) with varieties of JC from other areas of the United Kingdom. Unfortunately, I have no data on Manchester, Bristol or Birmingham, where there are major Black communities. I do have taped data, however, from Peterborough (in the East Midlands) and Nottingham (the North Midlands), which show that a form of Jamaican Creole is spoken in both these areas by British-born generations. To make a proper comparison, a well-conceived operation would have to be mounted to collect data in such a way that like was compared with like. This may sound simple, but the complexities involved in this case are enormous. Failing that, one would have to draw on the native-speaker intuitions of (say) London/Jamaican speakers, asking them to detect distinctive features in taped or actual speech from other areas. Looking at the data I have for five areas of the United Kingdom there appear to be no *obvious* differences. Patricia, for instance, has the full complement of Jamaican Creole phonology in her broadest style and so do broad speakers in London. At the same time, the slight shortfall from the broadest phonology exhibited by the Peterborough speaker is also typical of many Bedford speakers such as Moira (or Patricia in less than broadest style). No obvious grammatical differences emerge, though here one cannot possibly make a proper comparison – since a very large amount of data is needed – except between London and Bedford. Briefly, all the grammatical constructions mentioned by Bailey and others for JC are found in the London- and Bedford-sited varieties, but there are modifications and *additions*, which perhaps affect London and Bedford talk equally. When all is said and done, however, a native speaker needs to check points such as these. Pauline Christie (a Jamaican linguist at the University of the West Indies), for instance, unearthed differences mentioned below, some of which had not been noticed before.

Differences between 'Caribbean' and British JC

At my request, Christie kindly commented on the features of
Ballad For You, 'Jamaican Story' and a transcript of a tape
by Angela describing a fight. She summed up the differences
as follows:

(1) the frequent juxtaposition of broad Creole ('basilectal')
features with standard English ('acrolectal') features;

(2) the appearance of Creole features that are characteristic
of the Eastern Caribbean rather than Jamaica;

(3) the use of certain structures that would seldom (she
thought) be used by a Caribbean sited Creole speaker.

I have already mentioned Christie's first point as a very
prevalent feature that may be a characteristic of true bi-
dialectals speaking amongst themselves – at least where the
dialects are so far apart as to suggest a comparison with
bilingualism. Christie points to the incorporation of 'English-
isms' (not her term) into British JC. These are exactly the
kind of feature that a non-Jamaican investigator might miss:

BJC (Angela)	JC
mi neva si **so many** people	me neva si **so much** people
dem ready fi tearout **each oda** eye	dem ready fi tearout **wananada** eye

Angela's material was particularly full of such features. She
is mentioned in chapter 2 as the middle-class girl who at the
age of 14 had to stretch herself to attain the ability of her
group of Black friends in JC speaking-styles. Subsequently
she left school and started a career in nursing away from
home, in a largely white milieu. She attempted to reproduce
her old speaking style, in the account of this fight, when
being taped at the age of 19. By dint of such speakers, however, English idioms and even English constructions are
introduced into BJC. This mirrors the introduction of Creole-
derived constructions into 'English'. Interestingly, though,
Christie classes *Ballad For You* as 'authentic' Jamaican Creole
(with modifications from other Caribbean Creoles). Note,

harking back to the question of ranges, that Jennifer Johnson also speaks completely consistent standard English with no Jamaican accent.

On her second point – influence from the Eastern Caribbean – Christie cites **aint** as a general negator, as in:

You **aint** know anybody. [*BFY*, lines 61–2]

– and the use of *shi* for other than the subject. Jamaicans in Bedford mention this feature too, which is very common amongst British-born speakers in Bedford, and indeed in London.

Before considering Christie's third point, there are two relatively minor grammatical observations to be made that will lead back to the main thread. Judging from available data, BJC speakers have overwhelmingly chosen to mark the continuous with *a* (*im a sing*, *shi a sing*, etc.) rather than *da* or *de*, the country forms from the Western parishes of Jamaica, and to mark the past tense (that is, pluperfect for action verbs, 'past-descriptive' for stative verbs) with *di* or *did* rather than the broadest JC forms *ben*, *en*, etc.). Also, where the past continuous is marked by (*b*)*en* + *a* + stem in classic JC: *wi (b)ena sing*, there seems to be an avoidance of this form in BJC. Usually it is replaced by *woz* + stem + *in*: *wi woz singin*, although *did* + *a* and *woz* + *a* also occur: 'di man whey Chalice **dida dance** wid woman' (the woman with whose man Chalice had been dancing). However, one *ena* example has surfaced in a correction to a poem written by a pupil of Caroline Griffen at Tulse Hill School, London:

> inna bearding
> A mudder ~~was barting~~ er bieby one night
> The yungest of (her) ten and as smaal as a mite

To explain the circumstances in which this was written: the class had set out to write a standard English translation of the Cockney poem 'A Muvver was Barfing 'er Baby one Night'. One boy, a South-African Asian, translated it instead into Jamaican. Subsequently, this correction (and others) to his version were made by the 'experts in Jamaican dialect' in his class. The correction represents *ina* (or *ena*?) *biedin* (had been bathing). Perhaps the most significant point to notice about *ina biedin*, however, is the *-in* at the end, which is redundant.

This brings us to Christie's third point: features that probably do not occur in Caribbean-based Creoles. This redundant -in occurs in Bedford, Luton and London data, added to the very common Creole continuous form with **a** to form a blend:

> they went a-rolling, rolling [April – Bedford]
> dem start a-glarin' [Angela – Bedford]
> yuh know dem woman y'a-talkin to me about?
> [Freddie – Luton]
> who dat bwoy ah-whine-in himself . . . ?
> ['Jamaican Story' – London]

As such it looks rather like the British and American dialect construction – and in the case of the occurrence of 'went a-rolling' in April's story it is difficult to say which it is. (The old **a**-verbing form still occurs in Bedford and London playground rhymes, though not in ordinary white speech.) Christie states, however, that these blends are not typical of any Creole spoken in the Caribbean.

The continuation of non-Jamaican forms of language

The first generation of people from the Caribbean brought a rich variety language with them: the Patois of many different islands and territories, including varieties of French Patois, and also more standard forms of West Indian English, standing in a continuum relation with the rest. In Bedford, about 60 per cent of Caribbean people are from Jamaica, which reflects the overall proportion for the whole country, and the majority of the remaining 40 per cent are from Barbados and Carriacou (a small island off Grenada) with a sprinkling of Trinidadians, St Vincentians and Nevisians. So although there was some diversity amongst the Caribbean-born generation in terms of different Patois spoken, the scene was set for JC to become the dominant, indeed virtually the only Patois, of the succeeding generations – not forgetting the lingering influence of the Eastern Caribbean. Elsewhere in England there *are* pockets of resistance to JC. In communities where Jamaicans are out-numbered by another Caribbean group there is some indication from some areas that other forms of Patois are being passed on. This may be true of the Anguillans of Slough, the Antiguans of High Wycombe, the Dominican French Creole speakers of Bradford, the St Lucian French Creole speakers of Luton, and the Dominican and St Lucian French Creole speakers in certain parts of London. It is certainly true of children of Barbadian descent in Reading, where Barbadians out-number St Vincentians and Jamaicans. Below is a transcript of part of a thoroughly entertaining tape made by two young ladies (aged 14 and 15 years). Both were born in Britain, though Jennifer (the speaker in this extract) had been to Barbados for a holiday. Here she is 'role-playing' her grandmother welcoming her to the island in Bajan-style Creole:

Le' mi tel yu chil' yu gona like Barbados – it good. Yu-a like di mango
/ləik//Ba:bedəs/   /ləik/
an di breadfrui[t] i di cassava i evithing. Now here's a beautiful place.
/kasa:va/   /nɔu/
Yu si outside? it all nice 'n thing. Di wedda [weather] gon come down
/əutsəid/   /ɔ:l/nəis/
an di sun gon hit yu hard on yu back. Now all yu do's gid up ō di beach
/ha:rd/   /nəu//ɔ:l/
ã yu lie down an ge' a nice-nice suntan [suck teeth = 'huh!']. Dese white
/dəun/
people out here i don' sun tan, i ca:n' get a better one like wi [laughter].
Oh, I gon cook she up some good cùcú, man! Shi gon like it. Di bredf'u'
/əi/
an cùcú? It taste sweet – yu don' min'yu mudda. I had to learn yu
/do:n//məin/   /əi/
mudda how to cook breadfruit 'n' cùcú!
/hɔu/

cucu/a dish made with corn or cassava flour (cf. Yoruba **Kù Ku** – the
   part of the Indian corn where the grain grows, Crowther 1852)
cassava/West Indian etc. plant with tuberous roots; its starch or flour,
   bread made from these (*Concise Oxford Dictionary*)
suck teeth (kiss teeth, or chupse)/a disdainful – sometimes insulting –
   gesture, made by placing the tongue on the back of the teeth and
   sucking

Both the intonation and the pronunciation of the vowels in Bajan mark it out as quite distinctive. The most noticeable

sounds are /əi/ or /ɔi/ for the vowels in **nice-nice, I**, and so on.
This is very close to West Country English pronunciation.
/əu/ for **now** and **down** sounds similarly West Country. The
long 'a' in 'Barbados' is also striking because of its frontness
(that is, nearness to the standard sound in man) and tenseness.
Glottal stops, /d/ sounds and complete elisions all tend to
replace /t/ anywhere except at the start of a word or in
consonant combinations. Postvocalic -/r/ – that is, the pronunciation of 'r' *after* a vowel – is considerably more common
than in Jamaican.

Grammatically, too, Bajan is distinct. At a fundamental
level of analysis it is probably only slightly less broad than
broad JC. However, on the surface it appears to be considerably more English – Jennifer's text illustrates something close
to the broadest Bajan, I believe (formerly, or even now in
isolated cases, there may have been a broader form, comparable to JC). Compare these forms:

Broad JC	*Bajan*
im (fem., all cases)	shi (all cases)
im **a** mi fren	shi **is** mi fren
a-fight	fightin
mi/a (pronoun)	I ('oi')/a

Bajan, like many other Caribbean Creoles, marks the habitual
aspect of a verb by putting **does** before the main verb stem:

> He **does** mostly **wear** a khaki shirt.
> She **does be** always **quarrelling**.

French Creoles

It is to be regretted that French Creoles are accorded only
this belated, brief mention – partly the result of the lack of
French Creole speakers in Bedford. Varieties of French Creole
may eventually give way before English-based JC in Britain,
but there is some evidence that they, like Bajan Creole, are
being passed on to second and third generations, to some
extent, in some areas (cf. Rosen and Burgess 1980).

In grammar and idiom of the New World, French Creoles
are strikingly similar to the English-based varieties. They have

a range of copulas that are not exactly the same as JC copulas in distribution, but similar. The tense aspect systems are parallel, using pre-verb particles to mark progressive (**ka**), habitual (**ka**) future (**kale** – exactly translating JC 'a-go'), past (**te**), past progressive (**te ka** – compare JC 'ena'), and completive (**fin**, **soti**, etc.). Adjectives become stative verbs as in JC; nouns are definite, indefinite and generic, and so on. Below are four proverbs from Trinidad and a transcript of a tale of the supernatural related in two languages by a Lutonian 16-year-old, Bruno, originally from St Lucia. The transcript was made by a student in London, using a system of spelling that to some extent recognizes the connection with standard French.

Trinidadian French Creole proverbs

Travai pas mal; ce ziex qui capons.
(Work is not hard; it is the eyes that are cowards.)

Ce lher vent ca venter moune ca ouer lapeau poule.
(It is when the wind is blowing that we see the skin
   of a fowl.)
Deie'r chien, ce 'chien'; Douvent chien Ce 'missier
   chien'.
(Behind dog's back is 'dog'; But before dog, It is
   '*mister* dog'.)

Hai moune, main pas ba yeaux panen pou chaier
   dleau.
(Hate people, but don't give them baskets to fetch
   water.)

(Thomas 1969: 120–7)

The Burning Tree

Y te bor dise heures mwen aller en savanla, lai mwen wive bor bef mwen papa mwen te ka garde. Mwen way un pie bois ka bwile y te un go pie bois y te ka bwile. Mwen te du butte bor bef mwen; lai mwen tourner y pas teka bwile piece encore, y pas teka bwile piece encore. Mwen garde et lai mwen leve tet mwen, mwen way ka sorti en lai tet mwen et ka kleway con soleil la ka bwile! Lai mwen garde pa lai passer un tet mwen ec y aller en vil.

Bruno's English translation (given immediately afterwards):

It was about ten o'clock, and I went to the country, and when I look far behind behind the trees I saw this tree burning. It was burning badly, and I was standing behind ... next to this cow, because my daddy ... my grandfather used to look after cows, and I went out there to look after them for a while and this tree was burning, it was burning brightly. And when I turn around it was burning no more, and when I ... I lift up my head it was ... this light came up above my head, and it came fast, and when I look up it was bright and burning like the sun. And it went townwards.

Bruno gave the following glosses to individual phrases, orally, after telling the two versions:

French Creole	*English*
pass'aller tet mwen	came over my head
du butte borbef mwen	standing by the cow
mwen aller en savanla	I went to the country
y teka bwile	it was burning
y aller en vil	it went townwards
papa mwen teka tchen bef	my dad used to keep cows

French Creoles are spoken not only in St Lucia and Dominica and (mainly) by older people in Trinidad, Grenada and Carriacou – they are also spoken in Cayenne (French Guiana), Martinique, Guadaloupe, Haiti, Louisiana (USA) and in Seychelles, Mauritius, Réunion and Rodriguez in the Indian Ocean. It would be interesting for teachers to try the following folk song on their French Creole speaking pupils with suitable tact: such pupils may be ambivalent about affirming their own cultural identity separate from others, particularly those of Jamaican parentage. It is a nineteenth-century Louisiana song or rhyme (from Cable in Jackson 1967). Note that it is intentionally humorous, of course, and so there is no question of laughing *at* this piece of New World folk culture. It is to be pronounced as French – that is, the spelling is in the French tradition – except that the 'r' in 'tchere' is silent. The pronouns differ from the Southern Antilles versions in that **to** and **toé** are used as well as **ou** for English **you** (singular), and that **mo** is used as well as **mwẽ** (I/me/my).

Si to té tit zozo
Et mo-même, mo té fizi
Mo sré tchoué toé – boum
Ah! tchère bizou
D'acazou
Mo laimein ou
Comme cochon laimein labou!

(If you were a little bird
and I were a gun
I would shoot you – boom
Ah! dear jewel
of mahogany [cedar?]
I love you
as pigs love mud!)

CHAPTER 6

Sociolinguistics and Choice of Dialect

EARLY LABOVIAN SOCIOLINGUISTICS

At the beginning of chapter 5 I mentioned the way in which different people will vary their language according to situation, but with different degrees of 'broadness' or non-standardness, depending on their upbringing and background. Thus, to paraphrase Labov's words, a *careful* London taxi driver is likely to sound like a *casual* insurance salesman though they may both be Londoners and both be said to have London accents. Labov pioneered a way of studying this accent variation systematically in the early sixties, working on the dynamics of the New York accent. In a brilliant piece of work involving the taping of interviews with hundreds of New Yorkers in their homes on the Lower East Side, he showed how the accent variation that everyone intuitively knew was there could be pinpointed, measured, opened up for conscious inspection (Labov 1966). An example of this early Labovian method applied to the London situation would be to tape a sample of Londoners from a range of social classes, using a variety of styles of speech – from very careful (achieved by asking them to read lists of words) through to casual (achieved by a variety of means intended to make the speakers forget that they were talking to a stranger and being taped). Then the use of an obvious 'accent marker' like /h-/ dropping would be studied across the various taped interviews, and graphs could be plotted documenting the accent shifts in a convincing way. The most relevant aspects of this method are that it involves

counting the occurrence of particular sounds that are likely
to be monitored out (or in) during accent shift, and that the
researcher attempts to cause the speaker's accent shift by
altering the situation from formal to informal.

Labov describes formality as in effect paying attention to
the language one is using, monitoring the language as one
goes along. In job interviews, for instance, this kind of
formality comes into play and usually results in the use of
one's most careful style – and in this and related cases, careful
means more 'educated'. In writing, too, great attention is paid
to the language as one uses it and the resulting style varies
from fairly to highly formal. McLeod (1979) asked an inner-
city school class about their choice of language forms for
writing and informal speech:

I offered a ... list [of ways of saying 'he has none'] to a second year
class in a London secondary school (a typical London class: white
Londoners, black Londoners, Indians, Irish, Greek and some other
nationalities are also represented). I asked them to say which they
would use in writing in school, and which they would use in talking
to a friend outside school, result:

	writing	informal
He has none		
He hasn't any	2	
He hasn't got any	15	
He hasn't got none		2
He aint got none		9
He aint got any		4
E aint got none		1
E got none		

One boy added his own version; 'E aint got nothin'.

Labov's methods have been used successfully to plot
accent and dialect switching in Edinburgh and other British
cities and in several communities in the Caribbean. The interesting thing is that this Labovian methodology did not work
when applied to the younger Black community of Bedford
during the Bedford Survey (Sutcliffe 1978). The sample of
children answered questions *on* English (the most formal
situation), retold 'English' stories, and Anansi stories, had
casual conversations with and without the researcher present –

all to little avail. None of these techniques caused the children to adopt a significantly more Creole way of speaking. With this particular community the normal tricks used for tinkering with the situation would not bring about a shift towards Creole because such a shift would be largely a conscious one for them, and also because their pattern of dialect choice cut across our simplistic notions of formality and informality. With hindsight (or more native-speaker insight at the time), a suitable situation could have been set up that would have elicited Patois.

The way in which patterns of Black British language choice run counter to the white pattern in the larger community is shown quite plainly by an inquiry into language/dialect selection carried out by Hadi (1977) in the West Midlands. In this she asked 108 first-year children at a local secondary school (68 indigenous British, 22 West Indian and 18 Asian) about their use of language. All were asked whether they changed from the way they spoke with their friends when speaking to certain adults (the headteacher, the milkman, the doctor and the school dinner ladies). The results for the 'British' and 'West Indians' are shown in table 6.1. The West Indian pupils changed their way of speaking for all these adults. Hadi wonders – informally – whether this means that they lacked confidence in the way that they spoke. It would

TABLE 6.1 *British and West Indian use of language*

Interlocutor		West Indian	English
Headteacher	No change	1	16
	Change	16	47
Milkman	No change	3	48
	Change	15	14
Doctor	No change	2	19
	Change	15	42
School dinner ladies	No change	2	32
	Change	13	26

Source: Hadi (1977).

not be surprising if it was found that they did, considering the various negative forces deployed against their identity and language, which Hadi poignantly calls 'a language without a name'. In fact the situation is most complex, but Hadi's interpretation is not inappropriate.

Eventually in the Bedford Survey work on dialect choice, a British-born Black girl showed just how irrelevant our Labovian approach was here. She actually asked whether we wanted the Anansi story told in English or in 'Jamaican'. The latter was agreed upon and the Anansi story reverted, on her lips, to something like the same dialect in which it had been printed originally (in the source book from which it had been translated: Jekyl 1966). But her use of JC here was the result of a conscious choice. Clearly a change of approach was needed.

INSIGHTS INTO DIALECT CHOICE

From this discussion it should be plain that there are ways of eliciting the speakers' own insights into language use that can then be used to build up a coherent picture. Whether what speakers say they do linguistically is what they actually do, constitutes another question. People are sometimes notoriously bad at recognizing their own speech habits, as George Eliot ironically reminds us when she portrays the innkeeper in Adam Bede as being unaware that he himself uses the 'dileck'.

Some of the young people had much to say about language choice, although their interest in the subject conflicted slightly with a certain reticence (there is a proverb 'talk half lef half' – 'only say half of what is in one's mind'). Quite fine discriminations between different dialects were made. Dorita for instance, a Trinidadian girl in her early teens, saw herself as speaking four different dialects on the English-based Creole continuum and also claimed to know a little Trinidadian French Creole.

Dorita: You-all born West Indian. When you deh [are at] home, you talk you West Indian, and you talk you English. Me, gyal, I talk in the West Indian as wil' as I could. I mean ...

Sharon: You don't talk English Dorita.

Dorita: Well, a said a don't like the English talkin'. A more like mi Merican talkin', my Trinidadian talkin', an my well, you know, mix up wi' the West Indian. Is hear you-all hear me talkin' [scornfully mimicking a 'refined' English voice]: 'I like to have a cup of tea, please.'

I know from other taped evidence that Dorita does use all these varieties, including 'Merican', though very little 'English talkin' – something she seems to reserve for mimicry.

The fundamentals that emerged from such talk, however, mainly concerned the balance of choice between *Creole*, of whatever variety, and *English*. One can generalize and say that these bidialectal speakers were quite sensitive to the contexts in which language was used – that is, social situations and their locations or settings: church, school, home, the playground, youth club, and so on. Yet Creole was to them most importantly a stylistic choice that could override the dictates of the situation, or rather create new situations – perhaps better described as events. What seems to happen is that dialect choice shapes/is shaped by the event in a dynamic way. A very straightforward illustration is provided in figure 6.1, where conflict as an event, or (say) 'cussing off'

FIGURE 6.1 *A reported pattern of dialect selection (Bedford Black community)*

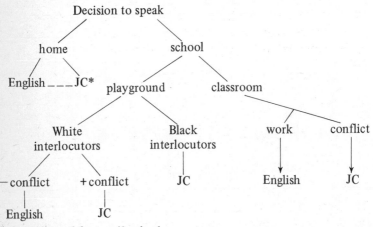

* Complicated factors involved.
Dotted line indicates continuum.

as a style, bring about a shift towards Creole, overriding the normal choice of dialect for the situation.

This figure, based on discussions with girls at John Bunyan School, Bedford, is incomplete even within its own simple terms of reference. Choice of just JC in the Black peer group situation is a simplification on the part of the girls, and the section of the diagram showing home use is a simplification on my part. The girls' collective perception of usage at home was summed up in the comment '*plien* English – and sometimes Jamaican' (and the dotted continuum line between the two varieties shown in the figure is a visual representation of this). Various happenings that could bring about a shift into Creole were mentioned, including 'talking to my Grandma about some of these teachers'. But by and large the consensus was that children tended to use English at home, while parents very often used 'Jamaican', especially when old friends came visiting.

THE BEDFORD QUESTIONNAIRE

During the Bedford Survey a questionnaire was devised so that this kind of reporting could be gathered in a more systematic way, yielding quantifiable results across a sample of local West Indian children of the first and second generation. The subjects (47 children and adolescents in Bedford and Luton) were asked how often Creole was used in two settings: home (divided into three situations) and the school playground.

Home	*School*
(1) Their speech to brothers and sisters.	(1) Their speech to Black friends in the playground.
(2) Their speech to parents.	
(3) Parents' speech to them.	

The subjects answered by indicating one of the following rates of use: always, often, sometimes, never. Obviously 'often' and 'sometimes' are totally vague words, but in the circumstances this did not matter. The words provided a sliding scale by which the situations could be scored for the sample, to yield scores of relative use of Creole – 'always' scored 3, 'often' 2, 'sometimes' 1, and 'never' of course scored 0.

Various objections could be raised – the complexity of the situations on which the questions were asked, the imprecise terminology – but in fact this procedure is sound as far as it goes, though admittedly the sample size was small. Subjects were asked for impression marking on use of Creole or Patois – a variety that as we have just seen does seem to have a fairly defined existence for the community.

TABLE 6.2 *Use of JC in four situations for the overall Bedford/Luton sample (expressed in weightings)*

To brothers and sisters	To parents	From parents	To Black friends (playground)
119	96	171	158
LOW	LOW	HIGH(ER)	HIGH(ER)

Table 6.2 shows the weightings that resulted for the four situations. The results emerge as surprisingly clear-cut considering the small size of the sample. If the sample is subdivided into younger (8–12), older (13–16), Caribbean-born/British-born, and so on, a similar pattern of results emerges. The subjects' own rate of use of Creole is highest in the peer group situation – to Black friends in the playground. Parents' use of Creole to them, however, is as high if not higher. Subjects' own use to parents is low. The score for use to brothers and sisters is usually intermediate or low. As we shall see below, it might well have been useful to ask for use to younger brothers and sisters separate from use to older ones. Hadi administered a version of this questionnaire to her own sample of 22 West Indians. She, too, found that a high use of Creole was reported for the peer group situation: 19 out of 22 of these first-year secondary pupils said they used Creole in this context. More will be said below on these figures and their possible cultural interpretations.

The Hadi and the Sutcliffe questionnaires attempted to find out what percentage of the sample was able to speak Broad Creole. The test sentence used in both (since the former questionnaire was based on the latter) was the Jamaican Creole: *mi asks di man fi put mi moni iina him pakit* (I asked the man to put my money in his pocket). Subjects were asked to translate it and were asked: 'Do you sometimes speak like that?' A surprising number in both surveys said that they did – 73 per cent and 78 per cent respectively. Similarly, over 90 per cent in each survey reported using at least some Creole. Both these small-scale surveys were carried out completely independently in two different areas of England. However, they used similar methodology and arrived at similar results.

The Survey of Linguistic Diversity in London Schools, carried out by Rosen and Burgess (1980), used a somewhat similar methodology – basically asking the speakers about their own language use – on a much larger scale, and came up with completely different results. However, they cast their question on use of Creole in a different form, and the most reasonable hypothesis is that this is what elicited such a different response from their sample. A less reasonable hypothesis is that the Hadi and Sutcliffe samples were alike in being composed of individuals who were much more likely to use Broad Creole. The discrepancy is valuable in that it highlights two different aspects of what may basically be the same phenomenon of language competence.

The crucial figures from the table in the Survey of Linguistic Diversity, presented as percentages of the total number who used any Creole features, are as follows:

	Jamaican	E. Caribbean
A full overseas dialectal speech	4%	2%
Basically a London (or standard) speaker though incorporating some overseas dialectal features	96%	98%

It is commonplace that Black British speakers do not sound like those brought up in Jamaica. They use much more of the

English end of the continuum, their English variety of speech usually predominates – basically a London/Bedford/Black Country (or standard) speaker – and when they speak Patois it does not sound quite the same as any Caribbean variety. This phenomenon in London has given rise to the term London Jamaican. So it is suggested that what we have in all three areas are West Indian populations where the rising generation, although speaking the local variety of English to varying degrees, are also able in the majority of cases to broaden Jamaican features in their speech to a point where it becomes Patois, a variety squarely in the Creole half of the range. At the same time, this Patois differs from the original Caribbean variety in ways that have still to be pinpointed.

HOME/STREET CONTRAST

The difference between language use in the home and the peer group settings, indicated quite strongly by the discussions and the questionnaire result, is mentioned in the literature on Black American language and culture:

A strong distinction, often discussed by young Blacks, is made between the kind of talk appropriate to the house when 'around moms' and that of the more public and open places where what some refer to as *street talk* may take place ... Talking is considerably more restricted in the house as to the subject of discussion, the vocabulary used, the amount of noise generally permitted to emanate from residents of the house, and the communication relationships pursued in that ambiance. [Abrahams 1976: 37]

This kind of finding can be generalized to West Indian households as well. Note that in parts of the Caribbean 'meckin' noise' is the term used to describe flamboyant use of 'street' forms of Patois. But from the evidence of the questionnaire and the various discussions, it emerges that Black *parents* in Bedfordshire have no such restrictions on their speech at home. They may use a great deal of Patois to their children, yet generally expect to be answered in 'English'. The position is asymmetrical but one that is generally endorsed by the community as proper. If children use obviously Creole speech in this context they risk being thought 'facety' (cheeky), at least in many households. Conversely, parents frequently use a broad and powerful style of Creole to chastise and control their offspring, or just to voice their anxieties and vexations. Once again this tendency is mentioned in Abrahams; it is a cultural trait running through Afro-American societies from Harlem to Surinam. Mothers particularly are seen to be adept at reducing chaos or 'rudeness' to order by means of skilful use of language. Although they can talk sweet, they know how to talk 'tough' or 'cold' with anyone who might threaten their self-image (Abrahams 1976: 63). In this context, **sweet** means, amongst other things, standard (where **tough** means highly non-standard).

There is now a great deal of accumulated evidence on the way this role is played in a British setting: direct evidence on tape, anecdote, role play, printed stories such as those of Jennifer Johnson, Jamaican dialect drama, and of course actual experience. The West Indian woman as Mother emerges as a formidable figure, whose ability to tongue-lash, or 'cuss off', is in no way to be taken lightly. An interesting aspect of this is the phrasing and imagery that is learned with the role. Even the Surinam example in chapter 1 is phrased in a style curiously similar to that of the mother in *Ballad For You*.

Mother: Whey you a dhu out yah? Is whey you deh?
Lorna: I was at the party, mommy, oh please don't beat me.
Mother: Noh beat you noh. Is what you was fighting ovah gal?
Lorna: Dem trying to teck whey my boyfriend.
Mother: You what? Man? You have man? Gal, you can't even wash you draws good an' a fight over man when you suppose fi deh a you bed. You have man. Well I going show you 'bout man you see, love.
[*BFY* lines 214–27]

It will not have been missed that this is an example of asymmetrical exchange: Creole from parent, English from daughter. When deferential use of English does not pacify her mother, the girl shifts towards JC to express her peer group concerns, which are of no consequence to her mother.

Of course, West Indian mothers do not all choose to play the tough role, or not in such a dramatic way, but typically they still maintain a dignity and a dominance with their children, and their children's respect and 'behaviour' is important to both parents. In Caribbean cultures as a whole, there is a strongly ingrained pattern of respect for one's elders. It goes partly unremarked because it is not part of the European-orientated official culture. In Britain, too, whites seldom seem to notice it. Nevertheless it is there. Consider the system of address in West Indian communities. Peers and those with no claim to respectability are very frequently addressed as **man** (both sexes), **guy**, **breda**, and so on. Anyone who is clearly older will usually expect title and surname: **Mrs** Thomas, **Pastor** White, **Missionary** Campbell. One may know an older West Indian person for years without being able to first-name them – in clear distinction from the post-war mainstream British system.

In the family setting especially, and also in other settings where Black people of different ages meet together, younger members are often reminded of their lack of age status and so kept in their place by comments such as the proverbial 'little sprat don't business in kingfisher affair' or 'you is a yout', 'big people talking', and so on. People show respect by their eye behaviours, too. Notice that eye behaviours are mentioned several times in *BFY*. However, the bold-face incident with the vicar is the important one to note in this connection. Granny Roach looks squarely in the vicar's eyes, making their eyes 'make four', and then she does not speak. Her bold-face behaviour is literally **facety**/*fiesti*/. All over the Afro-American world and in West Africa it is thought to be disrespectful to look too obviously into the eyes of an elder. This Black American comment is typical: 'Nobody with a smidgen of training, not even the worst roustabout, would look right into a grown person's face. It meant the person was trying to take the words out before they were formed' (Angelou 1971). A West Indian might put it this way: 'shi look slap in-a mi t'roat, teckout every word'. All too often white teachers in British schools who encounter this averting of eyes when they are talking to Black pupils misunderstand the behaviour, with unhappy results of course. Granny Roach's demeanour in this instance is a highly disrespectful breaking of the expected norms. This is the sort of situation that a self-respecting West Indian woman like Lorna's mother might take on with alacrity, even if she did not know the delinquent in question. In connection with disrespectful and typically peer group gestures, which like the respectful eye behaviour have fairly obvious African origins, we could mention sucking or 'kissing' teeth, and cutting eyes (not as painful as it sounds).

However, to return to the complementary roles of 'English' and Creole, English, or at least less creolized speech, has come to play a symbolic role in the cultural patterning I have been looking at. It is the language of deference, the 'vous' form. Creole, with its association with peer group, with feeling, with the genuine, is the 'tu' form. The hierarchic nature of this language use is maintained within the family even between younger and older brothers and sisters. This means that there are circumstances where an older brother will object to receiving Creole from a younger, but may shift toward Creole to tell him so – as of right.

Young people of course vary in their predilection towards Patois. There are some speakers who even as teenagers cannot be said to be able to speak it, even for mimicry. At the opposite extreme there are some, mostly males, who are said 'never to come out of it' and seem to be in the tradition of the Patois men of San Andres (J. Edwards *et al.* 1975). The kind of life-style that is chosen in mid-adolescence may have a clearly observable effect here. Two main life-style groups are mentioned by Crump (1979) and Troyna (1977) as relevant:

(1) Rastafarians and devotees of reggae;

(2) Soul-heads – devotees of soul music, whose orientation tends to be more 'conformist' to mainstream culture.

The second group are understandably regarded as less likely to speak Patois – but note that Lightening in *BFY* is a Soul-head yet speaks Patois. Another important group, which may overlap with the Soul-heads at least, is that of the Pente-costal Christians and Seventh Day Adventists. Many young people, and more girls than boys, are very involved in the life of the Black churches.

STYLE AND DIALECT CHOICE

For many speakers, Patois is the marked form used for special events and special tones: sarcasm, joy, anger, frustration, humour, irony and banter. Overlapping this is its use in a number of verbal performance styles or genres. This does not mean that Patois is infrequently used. Special effects and performances account for a prodigious amount of most Black teenagers' output, particularly in the peer group where 'normal' speech may constitute the troughs between the waves. Verbal performance here refers to particular styles of language that require extra skill and attention on the part of the speaker and the critical involvement of an audience, however informally gathered. A near-universal example would be telling jokes. Invariably a verbal performance can be evaluated, and perhaps retailed, by a new speaker. For 'performance' we could read 'drama' or 'dramatic style'. This drama/performance element can, incidentally, be faded in or out, and sometimes is only ambiguously present.

The heightened awareness of one's own language that obtains in verbal performance does, however, cause Black speakers to focus on one or other dialect. This is a kind of formality in the sense that Labov defined it – in terms of increased monitoring of one's speech. I would suggest that it is this that tends to keep JC stable and keep it from decreolizing, despite the tremendous variation.

The performances that seem inherently to require Patois are 'cussing' (and associated styles in which feelings pour out) and the common forms of verbal duelling known as tauntin' or cussin', and rhymin'. Tauntin' is a typical playground or street activity for pre-adolescents and adolescents, and is a distant cousin of Black American 'sounding' and 'woofing'.

The difficult, interesting question is what happens to language and linguistic culture (including the Opies' type of rhymes, songs and games and so on) when children from different cultures mingle together in the primary school playground. There has been only a very small amount of research on this. The question is brought up here, in connection with language selection, because of the role of Patois in verbal duelling. This is something that many Black children

indulge in somewhere between the ages of about 8 and 16.
Perhaps it follows naturally that if you participate in the
culture you indulge in verbal duelling at some time. But
what happens if you literally haven't the language for it?
There seems to be a 'low spot' on use of Creole between
around 4 or 5 years to around 9 or 10. What happens to the
language and language genres during this time? Do many
Black children retain their Patois just for verbal duelling?
(Rosemary Thomas has pointed out in a personal communication that she has a tape of a 7-year-old boy developing
JC in verbal duelling and word-play; cf. Thomas 1978 for
transcript.) This is an area that ought to be thoroughly
researched.

CONCLUSIONS

Overall, then, the dynamics of language use are most complicated. There is great scope for individual variation, where
individuals can impose their interpretation on a situation,
consciously selecting a dialect or playing with different
levels of dialect (as in Marcia's 'Jamaican Story'). Behind
this variation lies a complicated value system in which
English is not just a 'formal' language, or a necessary mainstream accomplishment for participation in the wider society,
or even a means of communicating in full with white class-
mates and playmates. It is also a part of the Caribbean
culture that these children have inherited and are re-creating
to suit their own particular needs in Britain. By this I refer
not only to the use of English in the West Indies as the
official language and the language of much middle-class and
educated life, but also to the role of 'English' (or less Creole
speech) amongst ordinary people in the showing of deference
and certain other specialized but traditional uses. Of course
both in the Caribbean and Britain one can use Patois to
symbolize (often dramatically) one's Black identity, or perhaps more exactly one's 'Afro' or 'Roots' identity. Already
the simplified picture I have attempted to delineate has
become complex and ambiguous. Perhaps the Western pen-
chant for analysis leads us to forget that we can analyse

without really understanding and understand without analysing. In other words, it may be that the best approach to an understanding of the subtleties of Black language use would be to hold back from dissecting and labelling and try instead to *appreciate*.

Texts

BROTHER HAANSI AND BROTHER BROWN

Jamaican derivation
Told by April – British-born, 8 years old
(spelling is standard where possible)

Once upon a time Brother Haansi [Anansi] and Brother Brown, they had this story, and Brother Haansi he went out and he picked some corn for his din-din. And Brother Brown said, 'Why don't you come with me to the grave?' And Brother Haansi said, 'No, no I won't.'

So Brother Haansi slept outside that night. And Brother Haansi saw this shadow like a doppy. And Brother Haansi scream out his head for Brother Brown. And Brother Brown came and said, 'What's the matter?' Brother Haansi said that he saw the shape of this doppy. And Brother Brown said that he will go and see what it is, Brother Haansi said 'aaright'. And Brother Haansi said, 'why don't you sleep out there too?' And Brother Brown said 'aaright!'

And the doppy came and saw Brother Brown, and he snatched the corn. Then in the morning Brother Brown went up into Brother Haansi's room and said: 'I don't see any doppy. Di doppy not dier. Di doppy is in i grave.' And Brother Haansi said that he would sleep out there the next night. And so Brother Haansi did sleep out there the next night. And he did see the doppy. He scream out to Brother Brown. Brother Brown come and lick di doppy pan im head. And Brother Brown thought that Brother Haansi was a doppy so he hit him with the pan, and he [Brother Haansi] fell asleep.

And so Brother Haansi woke up the next morning and said, 'What is this? You hit me pan di head wid di pan, and you hit di doppy with di pan, too. And you mek di doppy, di doppy lie dong pan di corn what I seed.'

But Brother Brown didn't take any notice and he went to town and he saw this donkey, so he brought the donkey and so the donkey did come with him. Brer Haansi said that he wanted a run, so Brother Brown said 'Aaright'. And Brother Haansi was going to go on the donkey's back, but he went by the tail bit. And so the donkey lif up his leg and kick him in i face. And he had one black eye and one red cheek.

And so one day Brother Haansi said that he was going to go swimming, and he saw this lady. She had a swimming costume on. And his eyes went curling round, and Brother Haansi wanted to kiss her. And the lady said, 'all right, you *can* kiss me.' And so Brother Haansi kissed her and fell on top of her!

And Brother Brown says: 'what is this? A Christian like you falling on top of a girl. And you say Hallelujah in church. And you not a Christian anymore, because I'm gonna tell the Pastor that you is not a Christian, yuh a a unsave'[1] [you are an unsaved person]. And Brother Brown felt very jealous of this and he wanted to do it himself, but he didn't.

And so Brother Haansi and the girl, they went a-rolling, rolling down into the sea. And a crab came and bite Brother Haansi pan him leg. Brother Haansi spring up as a light, and him rub him leg. And all the lizard come and bite-off him toe. And the girl said that 'I want to marry you, honey'. And so Brother Haansi said, 'All right he can, baby'.

[1] It is exceptionally unusual to have two a's together like this. That April has not 'deleted' or dropped one of them (effectively the second) can perhaps be put down to the fact that she is only 8 years old.

THE WITCH AND THE MORTAR STICK

Jamaican derivation
Told by David – Jamaican-born, 13 years old
(transcript spelling is standard where possible)

Once upon a time there was a boy and a girl. The boy was climbing up a tree. A lady came along.

'Could you give me an apple?'

The boy said 'Yes, catch.'

And the old lady said 'I can't catch.'

And so he said 'Climb the tree.'

The old lady said she can't climb.

And he said 'I'll drop it on the ground and you can pick it up.'

And she said 'No, the apple will get all dirty.'

And lady said 'Will you come down and give it to me?'

And when he came down the lady took him up and put him in a bag. And she carried him right round and 'wam!' – put him down, went to a shop, bought something. Two men saw the boy and let him come out, and put all sorts of things in the bag. And when she came back and was going home, she felt something wet coming down on her. She said, 'Well, you a pee-pee on me? Well I'll find out about you when you get home.' And when she came home she saw all muck and all pee-pee in it [the bag]. So she went back on her field. So she saw her boy on her apple tree. She said:

'Could you give me an apple?'

The boy says 'Yeah; can you catch?'

She says 'No.'

He said 'Climb the tree.'

And she said she can't climb the tree. 'Come on and give it to me!'

The boy came down and she caught him and carried him in a bag. This time she didn't stop. She went straight home. And when she went home she put the oven on and lit the gas to roast the boy. She put the boy down upon the floor. And while she was heating the oven she asked, 'Why is your hair so pretty?'

The boy said 'My mother took a mortar stick, and lick me in my head.'

And the witch said 'Would you use a mortar stick, and lick me in my head, and it come like that?'

And the boy said, 'Yes.'

And when the boy said that, that wasn't true – he wanted to kill her. And the witch unloosed the boy and gave him a mortar stick. And he gave the lady one lick in her head, and she died. And he put her into the oven.

THIN FOOT, BROAD MOUTH AND BIG BELLY[1]

Trinidadian derivation
Told by Dorita – Trinidadian-born, 13 years old
(spelling is standard where possible)

So one day the 3 brothers Thin Foot, Broad Mouth and Big Belly was walking in the field because it had a big puppah [paw-paw] tree, puppah tree right around and that is the onliest puppah tree that ever bear. And they ... when the brothers passing this man garden to go by their grandmother, while they was on the way walking, Big Belly was the onliest one that coulda climb up a tree. They send him up the tree because he was the biggest and he was the onliest one that could climb the tree. Big Belly climb up the tree and start eating the puppah, eating the puppah, eating the puppah, and he only sending down skin and seed, skin and seed, skin and seed for his brother.

'Please brother, send us down a paw-paw,' his other two brothers been call him ... So ... no! And he said, 'All he could eat those that I'm throwing down.' They said: 'Only skin and seed that you're throwing down.' He said, 'All he could still eat it.' And he keep on sending down the skin and seed. He start eating until his belly getting bigger and bigger and bigger and bigger.

[1] Compare Michael's Jamaican version of this story in chapter 5 and Akan versions – for example, 'Ashanti Story' (Morgue 1957).

So one day his brother-dem look for nails. And they found the nail and they take this thing, and while Big Belly was eating he couldn'ta hear they punging the nail in the pappah tree, and they know that was the side he woulda come down on. So they nail the nail-dem on the pappah tree. They said: 'Look, the man is coming.'

And Big Belly skid down the tree, and Big Belly split in two. Broad Mouth laugh. He laugh and laugh and laugh until his mouth split in two. Thin Foot run home to go and tell his mother and father that his other brother belly split and his other brother mouth split in two. As he go t' put his foot on his step his foot stick in a ants-hole, and when his father came, his father saw him, father said: 'What's the matter with you? Why you sticking your feet in a ants-hole?' said: 'I been here for more than ... 5 hours now Dad.' He said: 'More than 5 hours in the burning sun?' He said: 'Yes Dad.' So his dad pull out his foot and his foot so sprained ... He tell his father and dem with father brother. They sew up Big Belly belly, sew up Broad Mouth mouth, and they mend his foot. So all the brothers had been kind to one another at the ending.

MINIBO, MINIBATANI AND KAKARAJIT

Trinidadian derivation
Told by Immogen – Trinidadian born, 13 years old
(spelling is standard where possible)

Once upon a time there was a lady. She had three kids: Minibo, Minibatani and Kakarajit. She did not like Kakarajit because he was so skinny and had too many sores. And, one day, she got fed up with him around the house and she put him in a pen, and locked him up in there. It had this wolf, it was a hungry wolf. So everyday when they ate they used to leave all the bones and the left over food for Kakarajit. And every time *he* got this 'dinner' he used to leave it for the wolf; the hungry wolf used to go and eat it for him. And they were great friends.

So, one day, the mother had to go down the town, and she told the kids not to open the door because it got this wolf that roamed around the place. They said, 'all right'. When mum went to town the wolf came and said [wheedling voice],

'Minibo come here, Minibatani come here,
And leave Kakarajit one there.'

And they said, 'That's not our mum.' The wolf went to a blacksmith, and asked the blacksmith to pound his tongue flat. Then he went and started singing again. He was outside the woman's house, say:

'Minibo, come here, Minibatani come here,
And leave Kakarajit one there.'

And the kids said, 'oh, that doesn't sound like our mum's voice, that sounds like the wolf!' With that he went off again and he asked the blacksmith if he'd file his tongue a bit flatter ... So the blacksmith did what he asked. He went back again and he said [high, feminine, wheedling voice]:

'Minibo come here, Minibatani come here,
And leave Kakarajit one there.'

Speaking like a normal lady. So they opened the door, thinking that it was their mum. And the wolf came in and ate the two children up. When the mum came home from the town, the song that she usually sang:

[sings] 'Minibo come here, Minibatani come here,
And leave the other one there.'

She kept saying that all the time and Kakarajit kept saying 'the wolf ate them, the wolf ate them'.

And she kept saying, 'shut up'. She kept singing that song over and over, and Kakarajit kept telling her that the wolf ate them. And she gradually realised that the wolf did eat them. Then she went and took Kakarajit out of the cage, and fed him properly, got medicine to heal his sores. And he lived happily ever after.

PERSONAL EXPERIENCE NARRATIVE: THE BIG AUNTY KATIE

Told by Godfrey – Jamaican
(spelling is standard where possible)

And when me go me go under the black mango tree
and me sit-down on the tree
and me eat.
Me eat, eat mango til me belly full
and then me just go again
walk to the coffee piece in Gander
and pick-up the little chip-chips. Wood and little rabbit
    feeding and sugar cane, bans ...
and me go
and me meet piece of sugar cane ban some.
Me pick it up
and me kyah it go give the cow.
When me go me see some bird in the trap what I set
and me sit-down there
and me watch the bird
til when the bird go in the Chokie [snare] me draw i
and the string burst
when me going now to get ...
when me going up on the tree to get the bird
    Me nearly put me hand down on the bird.
The bird fly away
and gone.
I was very cross.
And I start to swear to meself
'Oh that bird get away
and me could have it to eat.'
And I go home with the feeding
and I put in the rabbit pen
an sit-down
and I go up back
and I fix the chokey, man
and me sit-down,
and me sit-down underneath the tree.
And I set a lot of Chokey on the tree-dem, apple tree
    and mango tree and all those lot

and sit-down
and I walk come go look lime
. . .
and pick coconut
and drinks jelly . . . water
and when I come down back I see a big Aunty Katie
    [Golden Oriole] into the stangerine tree.
And me take me time come down out the coconut tree.
Me never let the coconut drop.
Me pick it up
me hold it een me hand
and come down slide out the tree.
And when me come down
and go
me put down the coconut
and me see the bird neck in the thing
you know
and me draw i.
When me draw the bird . . . I tie the string onto the other
    piece of limb down at the bottom
and then me go up there
and me catch the bird.
But the bird didn't dead.
The bird pick me on me hand.
But me didn't let it go.
Me run home quick
and shout out
He-e-y! I catch a bird!
I catch a bird!
I catch a Aunty Katie, Aunty Katie, Aunty Katie.

VERBAL DUELLING

In chapter 2 several short examples of interactional verbal
performance were given. Many of these instances of word
pyrotechnics would be well described as verbal duelling, the
exchange of rhymed or unrhymed insults in a style known
as tauntin' or cussin'. The transcript below is of a prearranged
bout between a Jamaican and a British-born boy of Barbadian

descent (a small part of which appears in chapter 2). The performance is fluent, although other Black adolescents in Bedfordshire thought their style a little immature – the two boys were aged 13 at the time of recording. The language of *E*, the Jamaican, is very 'basilectal' or broad in places. *S* is less broad, and shows an underlying non-Jamaican influence in his pronunciation, although he seems to be aiming at producing Jamaican Creole. (Spelling is a highly modified form of standard.)

S: shut yuh dyamn bone-head, eh?

E: fi-yuh 'ead long like dem coconut.

S: Wha? Yuh favour pumpkin.

E: Yuh favour ... ackee.

S: Ackee?

E: Yuh see yuh 'ead dry [bald] like dem peel-'ead Johncrow [bald-headed crows]. Maaga [thin] skeleton bitch, yuh!

S: Who yuh a-bloody-call bitch? Yuh call mi bitch? Yuh look like somep'n from space.

E: Yu look like dem zombi.

S: Zombi? Yu look more 'an zombi.

E: Yuh look like dem gorilla, like dem monkey eena di jungle.

S: A gorilla got more sense dan wha yuh got in yuh head.

E: Yuh got any dyam sense a yuh?

S: Yeah. My head full wi sense, yours ...

E: Yuh touch my bro' n' a gonna, I gonna le' yuh have one fis' in yuh mouf, right?

S: Yuh touch mi an my broda gonna le' ... a gonna ram yuh one so hard yuh gwine fall on the ground.

E: Yuh broda weak like ...

S: Weak?

E: Weak like ... im naa have strenf ... im skinny like dem piece a grass straw, I jos touch him him gonna ...

S: Shut up an listen to me.

E: Yuh ain' tell mi to shu' up.

S: Mi di seh shut up an listen to mi!

E: No!

S: Yuh broda so weak, a touch im wid one finger an im drop on di floor.

E: Ma broda, le' mi tell yu somefing, bwoy! My broda kyan [can] trouble, beat up your brother, so shut yuh mouf, right?

S: Yuh wan' bet pan dat?

E: A bet dat yuh broda can't do nofing. 'E's weak like a fly. Dis bwoy down a park beat im up an im runaway ... chicken yuh.

S: Well wha 'bout yuh broda? Wha 'bout yuh broda? A bwoy smaller dan im lick im like wha! Lick! – im have a bleedin' nose, a black eye.

E: A donkey give yuh two back kick yuh fly to wheh yuh come from.

S: What about . . .

E: Yuh don' trouble mi broda again, 'cau' if yuh trouble him again, yuh gonna have . . . don' le' mi hit yuh now bwoy, tek a stone an bus' yuh 'ead fi yuh. A blin' yuh, a tek mi sling-shot yuh know, I blin' yuh eye fi-yuh, yu know.

S: Yuh think so?

E: Yes, mi know, man.

S: Bwoy, if a tek a catapult, bwoy yuh betta get outa range.

S: . . . 'cos when mi ready to aim, I will lick everything offa yuh. One shot an' cou' peel-off . . .

E: When y'a h'aim, yuh naa aim afta mi, yuh aim afta somep'n. But when a'm h'aimin', mate, mi a-haim afta yuh y'eye [I shall aim at your eye] . . . Dem big like dem frog.

S: Suppose yuh fling stone . . .

E: Yuh ears long-out like fi-donkey.

S: Weh yuh favour, dyam ostrich? Ostrich give yuh broda one kick . . .

E: Yuh nose a fi-dem gorilla [your nose is like a gorilla's].

S: Gorilla? Mi nose betta dan yours. Mi nice an' smood. Yours look like

E: . . . fi-donkey 'tickin' out like dat.

S: My ears nice an small . . .

E: . . . big like . . .

S: Big? Biga dan yours.

E: . . . long nose sinting [something, i.e. individual].

S: Don' argue wid mi bwoy.

E: . . . 'cau' yuh scrape-head, yuh dyam peel-head Johncrow.

Glossary of Linguistic Terms

Afro-American

Pertaining to Black peoples in the continent of America, including the Caribbean.

Aspect

Verbs in English, as in Creoles and very many other languages, show not only tense distinctions in the strict sense (time distinctions) but distinctions between completed and continuing actions, habitual actions and the like: **I did run, I was running, I used to run**. These examples can all be regarded (loosely) as representing different tenses; more accurately they are all examples of past tense but show different **aspects**.

Atlantic Creoles

See *Creole*.

continuum, the

This linguist's term refers to the range of language found in many Creole-speaking areas between an official standard language used especially in the media and in formal usage and an extreme form of the local Creole.

Copula

A verb with little meaning in itself that serves to link subject and predicate together: she **is** a teacher; the yams **are** delicious; the birds **are** on the wing; the swallows **were** darting. In English an important copula is the verb **to be**. Creoles have a range of different copulas equivalent to the verb to be – selection tends to be dictated by the kind of predicate that follows.

Creole (referring to language)

A new mother tongue brought into being through intensive contact between speakers of more than two different languages. It will be similar in terms of vocabulary to one of the languages involved, but show differences in grammatical structure. Creoles mentioned in this book are African or Afro-American in origin, and people who speak them often call them 'Patois'. In most cases they are spoken alongside more prestigious standard languages, of which the Creoles are often viewed (wrongly) as deviant forms. For example: Haitian Creole and standard (Haitian) French; Jamaican Creole and standard Jamaican English.

Creolist   A linguist specializing in the study of Creole languages.

diphthong   A succession of two or more vowels pronounced in such a way that they are not clearly separate sounds. For example /a/ and /i/ in 'night' /nait/.

Gullah   A Creole, quite similar to Jamaican Creole, that is spoken along the coastal strip of Georgia and South Carolina (USA) and especially on the offshore Sea Islands.

homophone   One of two or more words different in meaning but identical in their sound. For example waist/ waste in English; bay/beer/bear in some versions of Jamaican Creole, where they can all be pronounced /bie/.

ideophone   A 'picture word' – a single word that depicts what otherwise would necessitate several words or a whole sentence. African languages are particularly rich in ideophones describing sounds, movements, states and so on. The closest to examples of ideophones in English would be **'zip** goes a million!' or **vroom vroom, clunk**, **whoosh** and so on.

inflection   The adding of affixes – usually endings in the case of familiar examples in Latin or German – to show grammatical distinctions. Modern English has fewer inflections than Middle or Old English, but still retains plural -s, possessive -s, past tense marker -ed and so on. Creoles and the West African Kwa languages have very few inflections.

interjection	A word used as an exclamation of emotion and therefore, arguably, a kind of ideophone.
intonation	The melody of speech, adding meaning or innuendo that would have to be conveyed by punctuation (or a more wordy explanation) if the written medium were being used. See *tone*.
lingua franca	A language used by speakers for whom it is not a mother tongue as a common means of communication (as Esperanto was intended to be used). For instance, Latin in medieval Europe.
modal	An auxiliary verb expressing potentiality, probability and other modes. A peculiarity of English modals (shall, will, may, etc.) is that they show limited inflection.
oral literature	Seemingly involving a contradiction, this term has been adopted to refer to folk tales, ballads, proverbs and even more impromptu forms of oral art. The content and/or style of oral literature is transmitted orally, and it has its own standards of excellence.
Pidgin	(1) A 'makeshift' version of a language used in contact situations, for instance as a 'jargon' between traders.
	(2) A more developed and more stable language, originally born out of a language contact situation (as were Creoles), generally not spoken as a mother tongue. West African Pidgin is an example of a very developed Pidgin, which perhaps deserves the status of full language.
	Creoles are generally viewed as having derived from Pidgins.
phonology	The system of sounds used in a language; in effect the pronunciation, viewed as a system of sounds.
performance	In the context of oral art this term refers to a speaker's response to an audience (however informally gathered) beyond the normal requirements of clarity or utilitarian communication – for instance in the telling of jokes. This response,

in terms of special imagery, timing, rhythm and so on, is more or less consciously adopted by the speaker and evaluated by the listeners.

predicate

The part of the sentence that expresses something new about the subject, i.e. what it does or is. Sentences (or at least many of them) can thus be divided into subject and predicate:

subject	predicate
My love	is like a red, red rose
Joshua	fought the battle of Jericho
shi	*taakin fuulishnes*

remodelling

In the study of Afro-American cultures, remodelling refers to the process of taking over a piece of European culture and investing it with new (Afro-American) meaning while preserving the original form to a certain extent.

Roots/'Afro' culture

The fundamental culture(s) of Afro-Americans (in the West Indies and continental America). Much in West Indian life-styles can be explained as the result of a continuing interplay between the 'Roots' and European-derived cultures.

Saramaccan

A Creole spoken in the interior of Surinam (formerly Dutch Guiana) by the descendants of Africans who escaped from the plantations at a very early date. It is the only New World Creole that, to date, has been generally accepted as a 'tone language' in the African sense. Its core vocabulary is derived largely from Portuguese and English.

'simplification'

A language tends to become 'simplified' when it is spoken as a second language by a large number of people with little opportunity or incentive to learn to speak it like a native. In the case of Creoles and frequently with other languages, this involves a reduction of surface detail only, with the result that a wide range of tenses and other grammatical distinctions are generated in a highly efficient way.

Sranan

The principal Creole language of Surinam (formerly Dutch Guiana). It is English-based – that is, its vocabulary is drawn largely from English.

standard	The variety of language that, by custom, is normally used in formal education and the media, and that 'educated' people are expected to be able to use accurately.
stereotypes	In the context of social psychology, preconceived images of groups of people, ethnic or otherwise. Mental clichés, at best they are generalizations, often misleading and of course frequently unfavourable. For instance, there is a stereotype (perhaps now dying out) of women as bad drivers.
style	(1) A type of language appropriate to a particular social situation and setting.
	(2) More particularly, a variety of language use seen in terms of its imagery and overall structure developed for a particular social/ aesthetic purpose – for example, joking, narration, verbal duelling. (Also known as verbal style or genre.)
syncretism	The bonding together of elements from different languages or different cultures. In the context of Afro-American anthropology and Creole linguistics, syncretism usually refers to the bonding of African with European elements. To take a linguistic example, Jamaican Creole **se** can be explained as a syncretism between English **say**, Twi sɛ and Ibo **se**, since the English and African words overlap in meaning (**se** means either 'quote follows' or 'that' used as a complementizer). Compare the allied notion of remodelling (above).
syntax	The arrangement of the words of a language into grammatically dictated patterns (constructions).
tone	Musical pitch used in a language to distinguish between words and/or express grammatical distinctions, such as tense. A very large number of African languages are 'tone languages'. The Creole, Saramaccan, is also regarded as a tone language. It distinguishes, for example, between mì (low tone) 'I' and mí (high tone) 'me'/'my'.

Glossary of West Indian and British Black English

Listed here are some 320 words associated with distinctive (especially 'Patois') West Indian usage which may not be understood by the outsider, but which occur in the speech and writing of British Black people, or in the internationally-known writings of Jamaicans who have chosen to avail themselves of 'Patois'. Most of the words in this glossary can be viewed as deriving from Jamaica, or from the Rastafarian movement which links communities across the Atlantic and across the Caribbean with its Jamaican roots.

There are a few words which are perhaps new-coined in this country. To give some indication of continuity and change, vocabulary which the author has noted to be in use amongst British-born Black people in Southern England has been *asterisked*.[1] Of course, some of the most important vocabulary used by groups of young Black people will be localized and short-lived. This seems to be restricted to quite a small number of significant words – some of the terms for 'pal' for instance, and those relating to under-cover activities. All the same, it may well be that a constantly changing urban Black slang, incorporated both into 'Patois' (i.e. Creole) and more English varieties of language, is now growing in importance.

Marcia Smith (London-born) brought out this point when

[1] This does not *necessarily* mean that the asterisked vocabulary is not used in the Caribbean. Most of it is. For further information readers are recommended to consult the *Dictionary of Jamaican English* (Cassidy and Le Page) which was brought out in a revised edition in 1980.

writing about differences between her JC and that of her parents' generation:

I think the main difference is that the Jamaican of my generation relies heavily on slang. For example, (1) **dunseye** meaning money, (2) **bana-check** describing a black person who goes out with a white person, (3) **edge**, a 50p coin. As in the case of (1) and (2) there is no apparent connection between the word and its English meaning, that is to say it is not broken or corrupted English.

   Also it changes and shifts constantly. For example, (2) is already out of date. I would say the language of my generation is closer to the Rastafarian language than the native Patois of my parents' generation. My parents would *not* say **fahwud I di dunseye** meaning give me the money. [Marcia Smith, personal communication]

a* /a/

(1) I.*
(2) Progressive verb marker: mi **a** talk (I'm talking, I was talking).*
(3) At or in: **a** Dulwich (in Dulwich); to: go **a** shop (go to the shop(s)).*
(4) Is (used before nouns, noun phrases, pronouns): im **a** di leader (he is the leader), **a** rabbit food! (it's rabbit's food!).*
(5) Indefinite article: a si **a** puss (I saw a cat).*
Also used before question words, especially at the beginning of a sentence: **a**-wa? (what?), **a**-who? (who?), **a**-wepart? (where?).*
If tone is found in JC it will be found here in differentiating between these **a** words. Thus dem start á fíght (**a** and verb on level high tone) is clearly 'they started fighting' and not 'they started a fight'.

able* /iebl/

To be able to cope with, ready to risk. Generally used in the negative: a don't **able** fi yuh (I can't cope with you, you are too much trouble).

after /aafta/

(1) (Main) English meaning.
(2) Towards, at: mi fi shoot **after** yuh? (I should shoot at you?).
(3) Since (logically).

all* /aal/

(1) English meaning.
(2) Even: shi **all** cook French food (she even cooks French food).*

am /am/ — Object pronoun, third person singular or plural: 'him', 'her', 'it', 'them'. In the proverb: Snake seh, im ongli haffi lif up im head an 'oman tek **am** a tie up firewood (Snake says that he only has to lift up his head and a woman will tie up firewood with him).

Anansi, Anancy* /Anansi/ — The spider/man trickster of Black folklore in West Africa, and in the New World from South Carolina to the Guianas.

an t'ing* /an ting/ — And so forth, and the like.

argument /aagyument/ — Discussion, conversation.

aunty katy /aanti kieti/ — A golden oriole (species of bird, occurring in the West Indies, and a rare visitor to Britain).

aunty man /aanti man/ — Effeminate man.

Babylon* /babilan/ — Biblical image first used by Rastafarians. Refers to everything which is viewed as negative or destructive in Western society: the police (Caribbean or British), oppression, forces ranged against the Rastaman, exile (from Africa) in England or the Caribbean.

backayard* /bakayaad/ — 'Back home', i.e. Jamaica, etc.

backra* /bakra/ — Boss, white person. In Barbados, **Backra** Johnny (poor white).

bad* /bad/ — (1) English meaning.
(2) Very good, admirable, daring.*
(3) (As an adverb) very, thoroughly: im sik **bad**.*

bad-mouth /badmout/ — To insult, speak ill against.

baggy* /bagi/ — Girls' or babies' knickers.

bangle /bangl/ — (Can mean) handcuffs.

banner* /bana/ — Red, gold and green hat (i.e. hat in the Rastafarian colours).

bans /bans/ — Plenty (of), a great many.

bat* /bat/ — Moth. **Rat-bat** is bat (mammal).

bateau, bato* /batuo/ — Raft, river craft.

batty* /bati/   Buttocks.

ben, byen   See **did**.

bickle /bikl/   Food.

big-eye* /bigai, big-yai/   Envy, envious; greed, greedy.

bloodclot(h)* /blodklaat/   Obscene expression – cloth used as sanitary towelling.

bobandeh /bóbàndé/   Male erection.

bold face* /buol fies/   Cheeky, 'brazen'.

bottle-lamp /bakl lamp/   Lamp with a glass chimney.

bounce* /bouns, bongs/   To jostle, barge into.

bra, breh* /bra, bre/   **Bra** Nansi ('Brother' Anansi). Often used as a tag or mild exclamation adding emphasis: Lord God dem desert me, **breh**! Compare **sa**! and **man**!

breda /breda/   Brother.

bredrin* /bredrin/   (Singular or plural) Black brothers. One's fellows among the **yout'-dem**. Rastafarians also express this as **Idrin**.

breed* /briid/   To be pregnant.

bruk, bruk* /brok/   To break; broke; broken.

bubby /bobi/   Breast(s).

buck* /bok/   To stub (one's toe, etc.), to butt.

buckhead* /bokhed/   Meet, run into.

budum /budum/   The noise of objects tumbling on the ground, the slap of anything against a flat surface.

bush* /bush/   (1) Countryside. (2) Medicinal herbs.

bwoy, bway* /bwai/   Boy.

calaban /kalaban/   Trap used to catch birds (etc.).

calalu* /kalalu/   Leafy vegetables, like spinach.

cane row* /kien ruo/   Type of plaited hair style.

carry* /kya, kyar, kyari/   Take: **Carry** mi ackee go a Linstead Market.

carry-go-bring-come /kyari-go bring-kom/   Tale-bearer. Also used as a verb.

cata, cotta   See **kata**.

chalice* /chalis/   Pipe in which 'ganja' is smoked (Rastafarian usage).

chap-off* /chapaaf/   Chop through, sever: im **chop-off** di cow neck (he chopped off the cow's head, literally severed its neck). **Off** also means thoroughly; therefore: shi hair **chap-off** (her hair was 'all' chopped off, fallen out).

check(out)* /chek (out)/   Inquire into, notice, see about, manoeuvre a meeting.

chinee bumps* /chainii bomps/   Type of hair style (plaits tucked under).

chuh!, cho!* /cho/   An exclamation of impatience, irritation, disgust.

chokie /chuoki/   A snare (i.e. a loop) used to catch birds (etc.).

clear /klier, kler/   Light-skinned (of a West Indian), mulatto.

come /kom/   (Can mean) to become.

come in* /kom in/   Seem (like): shi **come in** jus' like a Jamaican (she seems just like a Jamaican).

company* /komp(i)ni/   People on friendly, equal terms: yuh t'ink seh mi an yuh is **company**? (do you (really) think I regard you as a friend/fit company?).

compe /kòmpé/   Equivalent, in many parts of the Caribbean, to Jamaican **bro**, **breda** (brother). Used as a title.

coo*   See **ku**.

cool* /kuul/   Fine, under control, pleasing: when mi un yuh first married, everything did **cool**, ennit? (things worked out fine, didn't they?).

(c)raven* /krievn, rievn/   Greedy, voracious.

crosses /kraasiz/   Hardship, 'trial'.

cruff, cruffty
/krof, krofti/
Untidy, rough, ugly.

cry /krai/
(Can mean) to mourn, cry for: a wouldn never **cry** dead fi yuh (I wouldn't mourn for you).

cups and saucers*
/kops n saasiz/
Type of hairstyle (plaits). Also known as 'flying saucers'.

cussin(g)* /kosin/
Tongue-lashing, tirade used to discipline children or put rivals in their place; adept, mock aggressive use of language.

cut-eye* /kot ai/
Insulting gesture in which one catches the other's eye and then pointedly looks away.

cut style* /kot stail/
To be fashionable, show oneself off, adopt a costume and bearing which is admired. **Cut** in several expressions means execute, perform. Note also 'pop style'.

cut ten* /kot ten/
To sit with legs crossed.

cut twenty*
/kot twenti/
To exaggerate, overdo.

da* /da/
(1) (Before verbs) Progressive verb marker (see **a, de**).
(2) **da ... de**, that: **da** night **de** (that night).*

dash-way /dáshwé, dáshiwé/
To squander, throw away.

daughter* /daata/
(Can mean) girl.

day clean /die kliin/
Dawn. Compare **day da light** in the Banana Boatsong (literally, day is lighting).

de, deh* /de/
(1) There.*
(2) To be situated (French se trouver).*
(3) Progressive particle before verbs: di monkey **de** jump, **de** jump (the monkey was jumping, jumping).*

dead* /ded/
To die, dead: mi **a** dead wi laugh (I'm dying of laughter).

deal, deal in*
/diil, diil in/
(1) To be concerned with, have to do with, relate to.
(2) (deal) practise witchcraft.

deso, dehso* /désò/
There, right there (emphatic form of **de** (1)).

dem* /dem/

(1) They, them, their.*
(2) Those.*
(3) The (plural).*
(4) (After definite nouns) plural marker: **di** gyal **dem** (the girls).*
(5) After names, **dem** means 'and company': Jane-**dem** (Jane and her crowd).*

dey deh, di deh*
/dede, dide/

To be (situated) there: mek sure yuh suppose fi **di deh** (make sure you're supposed to be there).

di* /dí/

The.

di ... dem*
/dí ... dém/

Sign of definite plural noun: **di** addah gyal-**dem** (the other girls). Compare: mi foot-dem (my legs).

diablesse, la diablesse
/jablés, lajablés/

A beautiful woman who haunts the roads at night, seeking to bewitch unsuspecting men. One of her legs takes the form of a cow's leg, concealed beneath her long white gown.

did* /did, di/

Past tense marker with 'state' verbs: I shoulda **did** know better (I should have known better). Pluperfect meaning with 'action' verbs: so he ax di wife if shi **did** wash di pot (so he asked his wife if she had washed the pot). **En, ben, byen** have the same meaning.

dirty, dutty* /doti/

(1) As a noun, earth, dirt: rain a-fall but **dutty** tough! (it is raining but the earth is hard).
(2) (Verb/adjective) to dirty; dirty.*

dis* /dis/

(1) This (emphatic form **disya, dis ... ya**).*
(2) Just (adverb).*

disgustin(g)*
/disgostin/

Irritating (of behaviour), annoying, disorderly.

do /du, duu/

Can be transitive, meaning to affect or harm.

doctor bird
/daktabod/

Humming bird.

does* /doz/

Pre-verb particle, showing habitual action: wa hurt eye **does** mek nose run (what hurts the eye usually makes the nose run) (proverb).

done* /don/

Finish: **lord-mi-done** (the workhouse).

dont, dont it*
/duont, duontit/

The equivalent of **innit**. Universal interrogative tag expecting the answer 'yes': Jack, **dont** is yuh? (That's you, Jack, isn't it?)

doo-doo* /duudu/

(1) Faeces.*
(2) To defecate.*

door-mout(h)
/duormout/

Doorway, space in front of the door.

down*- /doun-/

Prefix denoting negative forces: **downpression** (oppression) (Rastafarian).

dread* /dred/

Terrible, excellent, deserving Rastafarian approval.

drink off /dringkaaf/

To drink up, drink (it) all.

drunk* /drungk/

(1) Intoxicated.
(2) To intoxicate: di rum **drunk** me (the rum made me drunk).

dry /drai/

(Can mean) bare, bald: im head **dry** like dem peel-head Johncrow (his head is as bald as a carrion crow).

dry eye /drai (y)ai/

Coolly impertinent, or 'bold faced'.

dub* /dob/

Jamaican instrumental music with a reggae beat, over which disc jockeys can put their own vocal improvisation or toast.

dunny* /doni/

Money. Also occurs as **dunseye** /donsai/: **fahwud I di dunseye** (give me the money).

duppy* /dopi/

Ghost, spirit of the dead. 'Suckin' duppy': vampire.

Eh-Eh* /é-é, è-é/

Interjection expressing surprise, consternation, interest or satisfaction at a discovery, knowing insight and so on: **eh-eh**, im a talk Jamaican (well, what do you know, he's talking Jamaican!). Spoken with two high tones it can also be used to mean 'look out!', 'cave'. Compare the Liverpudlian expression 'eck, eck!'

en*

See **did**.

evening(*)
/iivnin, iivlin/

Afternoon until about six p.m. (followed by the 'late evening').

extra* /ekstra/   (1) Fussy, prone to object.
                                          (2) Boastful, self-assertive.

eye-water* /aiwaata/   Tears (sometimes shortened to **water**).

eyes* /aiz/   To look at, make eyes at.

facety* /fiesti, fiesi/   Cheeky, disrespectful.

fahwud* /faawod/   To give, advance (Rastafarian usage).

fas'* /faas/   (Can mean) nosey, meddlesome, impudent.

favour* /fieva, fieba/   To resemble, seem (like): shi fut-dem **favour** capital K (she is knock-kneed).

fenky-fenky   (1) Finicking.
(fengki fengki/   (2) Puny.

fi, fe* /fi/   (1) (Before a main verb) should: shi **fi** go (she should go).*
     (2) (Before the equivalent of an English infinitive) to: shi waan John **fi** kiss her (she wants John to kiss her).*
     (3) (Before noun/pronoun) for.*
     (4) (Before a possessive pronoun) sign of emphatic possessive: a **fi-wi** language dis (this is **our** language).*

fi true* /fi truu/   Truly, very: di gyal pretty fi true, yuh si? (the girl was very pretty).

foot* /fut/   Leg, including the foot. Compare **hand**.

fraid /fried/   To fear, be frightened of. Catch 'fraid (get/be scared).

frighten /fraitn/   (Can mean) Surprised: mi **frighten** seh im gi mi none at all (I am surprised he gave me any at all).

full* /ful/   To fill, full: mi go a riva go **full** a pan a water (I went to the river to fill a pail of water).

fufool, foo-fool*   Fool, foolish.
/fufuul/

-ful /-ful/   Can be added to many verbs to make an adjective: unu too **destroyful** (you (plural) are so destructive).

fum-fum /fom fom/   Beating, hiding.

ganja* /ganja/   Marijuana.

gi* /gi/
(1) Give.*
(2) (As last verb in a sequence) for, to benefit: daddy gwine skin yuh bottom **gi** yuh (Daddy will 'skin' your bottom for you!).*

good   In middle-class Caribbean usage 'good' in connection with hair, skin, or features often means European-type.

gourdi /guodi/   Gourd, calabash.

grounation*
/grounieshan/
A special gathering of Rastafarians for reasoning and celebrating their Rasta identity.

gyal* /gyal/   Girl.

guilty /gilti/   (Can mean) guilt. In fact, many adjectives (and verbs) can be used as abstract nouns.

gunguh /gunggo/   Pigeon peas (cajanus cajan).

gwan, gwaan*
/gwaan/
To carry on, go on.

gweh* /gwé/   Be gone, 'scram' (imperative).

gwine* /gwain/   Going, going to.

h* /h/
For many Jamaicans this is purely an optional extra, used for emphasis before any vowel: yuh too **hugly!** (you're too ugly/so ugly!).*
However, Jamaicans from Western Parishes, and most other West Indians use **h** more or less as in standard English, as do standard Jamaican English speakers.*

haffe, haffi* /hafi/   To have to, be obliged to: yu **haffi** go a shop (you've to go to the shop(s)).

hand, han* /han/   Arm, including the hand.

han' middle
/han migl/
Palm of the hand.

hard* /haad/
(1) English meanings.
(2) Of music, films (etc.): admirable, good, aesthetically pleasing.*
(3) See below, for figurative uses.*

hard ears* /haadiez/   Stubborn, disobedient.

hard head* /haadhed/ — (1) Stupid, dull of reason: coffee mek di **head hard** (coffee makes you stupid).
(2) Stubborn, disobedient.

heavy* /hevi/ — (1) (Can have a variety of positive senses:) original, pure, intense, interesting, redolent.
(2) heavy manners: heavy handed control, repression.

herb* /(h)erb/ — Marijuana, weed.

hurry-come-up* /hori komop/ — Nouveau riche. Also used as a verb.

i* /i/ — It; its.

I-and-I, I-an-I /ai an ai/ — I, the Rastaman's pronoun of individuality and collective awareness and interest. Perhaps also expresses the idea of God in/with the individual.

Idrin /aidrin/ — Fellow-Rastafarians, brothers.

ignorant /ignarant/ — Angry, showing uncontrolled anger.

im* /(h)im/ — He, him, his; she, her, hers; it, its.

ina, eena* /(í)íná/ — In, into, inside.

ing-hing* /iìng-híng, ēè̄-hēē̄/ — (1) Yes.
(2) Interjection expressing 'I told you so', 'there you are, then', 'would(n't) you believe it'.

innit, ennit* /init, enit/ — General purpose interrogative tag to questions expecting the answer 'yes': So, I ongli talkin' to her, **ennit**?

I-tal* /aital/ — Pertaining to food which Rastas believe not only fit to eat (i.e. without pork) but wholesome. Perhaps based on 'vital', this word is an example of many Rastafarian terms which play on the sound 'I' as the symbol of life-affirmation, and consciousness – as opposed to 'slave' unconsciousness.

J.A.* /jie-ie/ — Jamaica.

jah* /jaa/ — God, in Rastafarian terminology, embodied in Emperor Haile Selassie.

jam* /jam/ — (Of musicians) play together.

Jam-down*
/Jamdoun, dong/

(1) Jamaica.
(2) (jam-down) put down something heavy.
Figuratively: a gwine jam-down some music
le' dem hear-weh, yuh si. (... so they can hear!).

janga /jánggà/

Species of edible crustacean found in Jamaican
rivers.

jinal* /jinal/

Liar, dishonest trickster, rogue: Sunday **jinal**
(a preacher). Fool (to oneself).

jook* /juuk/

To pierce, jab, prick, poke; enter (sexually);
im **jook-off** mi eye (he (nearly) poked my
eye out!).

John Crow* /jankro,
janko, dranko/

Red-headed turkey buzzard; carrion crow.
Fabled for being very black, bald, voracious.
'Iron **John Crow**': aeroplane.

Johnny cake*
/janikiek/

In traditional Jamaican cooking, a kind of
dumpling or scone. Bakes.

John-Chewit
/ján-chùìt/

Black-whiskered vireo – species of bird found in
Jamaica, and elsewhere in the Caribbean, as
a summer visitor.

juba /juuba/

Unflattering term for a woman, middle-aged
'busybody', etc. Originally an African day
name (from the Akan language) given to girls
born on a Monday.

jumby /jombi/

See zomby, zombie.

kalalu* /kalalu/

See **calalu**.

kas-kas /kas-kas/

'Signifyin'' – rumour-mongering, character as-
sassination. Some speakers contrast this with
cuss-cuss, the act of cussin'.

kata /kata/

(1) Head pad to ease the head when carrying
a load.
(2) Comb or 'frizzle' of a senseh fowl.

kenge* /kengge/

(1) Yaws, sore on the legs (etc.).*
(2) Puny – as in the name 'Kenge-Foot' (?).
Cf. Yoruba: kéńké (puny).

kiss-teet(h)*
/kistiit/

To 'suck the teeth' with one's tongue placed
behind them – a familiar or disdainful gesture.

ku, kuh, khu* /kú/   See, look at (imperative only): **ku ya** (look here).

kuku* /kùkú/   Maize meal dish.

kwabs* /kwabs/   Companions, fit company* (see **company**). **Kwabs up***: to edge up (of children, trying to join in with a group of adults).

kyaan done* /kyaan don/   Exceedingly, infinitely (literally: can't finish): dat biebi ogli **kyaan done** (that baby is exceedingly ugly). Compare Black American 'won't stop black' (exceedingly black (skinned)).

kyan, kean* /kyáan/ ·   Can't.

labrish* /labrish/   (Noun and verb) gossip – relaxed, lively talk amongst friends: No bada **labrish** ova di phone no yuh know – a money (don't gossip over the phone – it's money).

lajabess, Lijah Bless /lájàblés/   See **diablesse**.

lackah, lakah* /láká/   Like, as (in comparisons): dat hard **lakah** rockstone (that's as hard as rock). Also occurs as like-a /láiká/.

lick* /lik/   To beat (i.e. spank, fight, etc.), hit.

lick-off* /likaaf/   Knock off: no **lick-off** di plate (don't knock off the plates, i.e. on to the floor).

licks* /liks/   Beating (noun). **Irielicks** /Airiliks/: (1) Hard luck.* (2) Beating.*

lickhead* /likhed/   To meet, meet up with.

longout* /lang-out/   To stick out (of tongue), extend. Extended.

lover's rock*   Slow sweet reggae with a lighter beat, and generally with female group providing harmonies.

ma* /ma/   Respectful form of address to older woman or mother. Also occurs as 'mom'.

maagah,* mawga /maaga/   Skinny, meagre.

manners* /manaz/   Respectful behaviour: Lord, shi have dem whites pan shi road undah **manners** (i.e. showing a healthy respect, or under control).

mart(h)a warren*
/maata waarn/ — Aggressive woman.

mashate* /mashiet/ — Cutlass, machete – heavy, broad knife used for cutting cane (and many other purposes) in the Caribbean.

mash-mash*
/mash mash/ — (1) (Noun) small change, odd change, etc.: four foot an **mash-mash** (four feet odd).
(2) (Adjective) messy, broken up.

mash-mout(h)*
/mashmout/ — (1) Shape of mouth associated with whites.*
(2) Toothless(ness).

mash up* /mashop/ — (1) To destroy, smash up, ruin (completely). (Of a marriage, relationship) to break up. (Adjective) destroyed, etc.*
(2) Unwell, in a poor way; untidy.*

massa, maassa,* maas'
/masa, maasa, maas/ — Master; Sir. Respectful title: **Maas** Joe.

mattah* /mata/ — (Can mean) 'sleep', i.e. mucus, in the eyes. Also **(y)eye-mattah**.

matty /mati/ — Friends, 'mates' (more typically used in the Eastern Caribbean; in Barbados especially used of women).

mek* /mek/ — (1) To make.*
(2) Let: **mek** a tek dem one by one* (let me take them one by one; I think I'll take them one by one).
(3) So that (result): mi no have-on mi shoes **mek** yu t'ink mi kyaan run (I haven't my shoes on, so you think I can't run).*
(4) Why (?).*

mek four* /mek fuor/ — Make 'four eyes', that is, to meet someone's gaze, look into each other's eyes.

mi* /mi/ — I, me, my. A pronoun avoided by Rastafarians in favour of **I**.

mind, min'* /main/ — (1) Mind (noun). Note the following: Mi mind tell mi (something told me ...); Shi no have di **mind** fi put dem back (she did not want to put them back).*

(2) Beware lest: **mind** yuh bruk down di wall (careful you don't break the wall down).
(3) Be sure to – opposite in meaning to (2). Difference marked intonationally perhaps.*

miserable* /mizeribl/   Rowdy, quarrelsome; miserable.

mouta massy*
/mouta masi/   Chatterbox, gossip, busy-body.

mout(h) water*
/moutwaata/   Saliva.

muma, mumma*
/mumá/   Mother (also **mama**). The traditional term of address to mother or older female is 'ma' or 'mum'.

naa* /naa/   **No + a** becomes **naa**; so the negative of **dem a pay** is: **dem naa pay** (they are not paying). See **a** (2).

name* /niem/   (As a verb) to be called.

nana* /nánà/   Grandmother (term of address).

na'si* /naasi/   Unwashed; improper, sexually 'rude'.

-ness* /-nis/   Ending which can be applied to many adjectives to create an abstract noun, e.g. **proudness** (pride).

nex'* /neks/   (Can mean, as adjective) another, different.

nine night /nainait/   Wake for the dead.

noh* /no/   (1) Not.*
(2) Meaningless particle in an emphatic positive statement: **noh** di vicar! (the vicar himself!).*
(3) (At the end of a sentence) Won't you?: cry **noh** (won't you cry?).*

noh business*
/no biznis/   Not to care about: dem **no business** bout dat.

noh muss* /nó mós/   It is inevitable, it must be.

noff* /nof/   Enough, plenty.

nyam* /nyam/   To eat, devour.

obeah* /òbíà/   Witchcraft.

obeahman*/òbíàmàn/   Exponent of witchcraft (male).

'oman* /úmàn/	Woman. Frequently used in compounds: **'oman** rain (drizzle); **'oman** god (goddess).
ongle, ongly* /ongl, ongli/	Only.
-off* /aaf/	Verbal particle indicating completion: drink-**off** (to drink up), and so on.
one* /wan/	(1) Numeral: one.* (2) Indefinite article; a.* (3) As an emphatic: is **one** piece a ting gwaan (it all happened! literally, is one piece of thing went on).* (4) Alone (especially after a personal pronoun): mi **one** an' God! (me alone, and God!).*
one-one* /wan-wan/	One here, one there, scattered. Also /wani-wani/.
old-head /uolhed/	One of the older generation, an elder.
overstand* /uovastan/	Understand (Rastafarian usage).
pan* /pàn/	(1) On.* (2) Any vessel used for cooking, carrying water, etc.* (3) Pond.
Patois* /patwa/	Creole speech (English or French). The former is also known as 'Jamaican', 'our language'.
peelhead* /piiled/	Bald, bald headed individual: **peel 'ed** Jankro (buzzard).
penetrate* /penitriet/	To understand through insight or deliberation.
pumpan* /pumpan, pempan/	A deep tin or vessel used for cooking, etc.
pickney* /pikni, pikini/	Child, particularly a little child. Young of animals. Often in compounds: **pickney gyal** (girl).
piki-piki* /piki-piki/	(1) Descriptive of hair cut to a short nap, spiky. (2) Finicking, 'picky' over food.
pop, pap* /pap/	(1) To break, snap, perform (something): **pap** two move (dance).* (2) Porridge.

poppy show* /papishuo/ — Ridiculous display in public, 'scene'.

pork* /puok/
(1) Pork, forbidden by Rasta belief.
(2) Whites – those who eat pork.

porkhead /puoked/ — White person; one who eats pork.

prugguh /prúgò/ — Species of edible crustacean found in Jamaican rivers.

puppah* /pupa/ — father; God. **Puppah** sa: Respectful address to father or older male.

puppahlick /pupalik/ — Somersault.

pure* /pyuor, pyuur/ — (Before nouns) only (= alone): not'n but **pure** style (nothing but style alone). Compare **soso**.

pumpum* /pumpum/
(1) Swelling.
(2) Female genitals.*

Quatty* /kwati/ — Penny-halfpenny (a traditional Jamaican unit of reckoning).

Quashie /kwashi/ — Fool, country bumpkin. Originally an African day name (from Akan) given to boys born on Sunday.

raas, rarse* /raas/ — Swear word, considered particularly obscene.

raasclot(h)* /raasklaat/ — An obscene swear word. Cloth used for sanitary towelling.

ram /ram/ — The male of the species: **ram**goat, **ram** pus (tomcat).

rata /rata/
(1) Rat.
(2) Bulging biceps.

rebuke /ribyuuk/
(1) (Of 'duppies' or ghosts) exorcise, tell to go.
(2) To condemn another while in the spirit/talking in tongues.

red* /red/ — In Caribbean folk cultural reference **red** tends to refer to shades of yellow orange or brown as well as red: **red**-skin man (light-skinned Afro-Caribbean man).

red eye /red (y)ai/ — Jealous.

renk* /rengk/
(1) Impudent, cheeky, 'wild'.

	(2) Smelly (as of unwashed things and people). Compare American 'funky'.
rhythm* /riddim/	(1) English meaning. (2) Movement of the hips in dancing (etc.) frequently seen as provocative or vulgar.
rice an' peas* /rais an piiz/	A traditional Sunday dinner favourite for West Indians, from rice, coconut oil and red beans. Compare Black American red beans and rice.
river maid /riva, riba, ruba mied/	Legendary female river monster or deity of Jamaica. Those who claim they do not eat fish are safe from the river maid. Others should beware, since fish are the river maid's children.
rivermuma /rívá, ríbá, rúbá mùmà/	A river maid (see above).
rockstone* /rak(a)stuon/	(1) Stone, pebble. (2) Exclamation: **rockstone** Anansi!
rolling calf* /ruolin kyaaf/	In Jamaica a mythical beast with fiery eyes, 'rollin'' or dragging chains. Said to be the ghost of a butcher, it menaces the country roads. If, however, you draw the sign of the cross at a crossroads you can delay its pursuit of you. It then has to return home and back seven times before it can proceed.
roots* /ruuts/	Pertaining to the 'Afro' or folk culture of the Caribbean: naa cut no style, a stric'ly **roots** (I'm just 'country'/good and country).
rub down* /robdoun, robdong/	(Of a couple) to dance together closely.
run* /ron/	(1) Can be used transitively, meaning to chase: di man **a run** mi down. (2) 'Di man a **run** mi down' (the man was arguing with me/telling me something).*
sa, sah* /sa/	Sir. Often used in exclamations: mi gone **sa**! (I'm off!)
sake-a* /sieka/	Because (of), since (logically): mi couldn' go a grong **sake-a** di time so wet (I couldn't go to the fields since it was so rainy).

scank, skank*   (1) To do (a specific) dance to a reggae base
/skangk/   line.
                  (2) To 'cut style', perform something with
                  urban panache.

school-mout*   School door; space in front of the school.
/skuulmout/

scrape-head*   Bald headed or short-haired.
/skriep-hed/

seed* /siid/   (Can mean) testicles.

seen!*, scene! /siin/ Agreed! 'Right on!'

seh, se* /se/   (1) Say.*
                  (2) A word indicating that a quote is to
                  follow.*
                  (3) Clause introducer, virtually the equivalent
                  of **that**: a glad **seh** im gaan (I'm glad that he
                  has gone).*

selfish /selfish/   Self-conscious.

shame* /shiem/   (1) To be ashamed; to shame.*
                  (2) (Noun): tek di **shame** an' don't complain!*

sick /sik/   Can be transitive: di coffee **sick** mi (the coffee
                  made me sick).

sight* /sait/   See, perceive.

sinting* /sinting/   (1) Something.
                  (2) (An) individual, a thing.*

sipple /sipl/   (1) Slippery.
                  (2) To make slippery.

sipplejack*   Whippy cane.

skinteet'* /skintiit/ To show teeth without smiling; give a 'plastic'
                  smile.

slack* /slak/   Of 'loose' morals.

so so!* /so so/   (That's) how it is.

soso* /suoso/   Lone, sole, solely.

soucouyen /sùkùyén   A blood-sucking witch who leaves her skin at
súkúnyà, súkúyè̀/   home when she goes about her evil business.
                  In Jamaica she is known as the 'Old Hige'
                  /uol haig/.

soun'* /soun, song/   Sound-system, discotheque equipment; the entire outfit, including the disc jockey.

spar* /spar/   Friend, pal. **Star** also occurs.

spliff* /splif/   Marijuana cigarette: build a **spliff** (make a marijuana cigarette).

(s)tan'* /tan, stan/   (1) Verb 'to be' after 'how' or before 'so': yuh know how Black people **stan** (you know how Black people are).*
(2) To remain.*
(3) Exclamation of surprise or sudden realization.

stay* /ste, stie/   Same as **(s)tan** (1) and (2) (see above).

suck-teet(h)* /sok tiit/   The making of a sucking noise with the tongue placed behind tongue, to express disdain, disbelief (etc.). Occurs also as **kiss-teeth**. Mi dida go talk to yuh, but tru yuh **suck** yuh **tiit** at mi, mi neva bada (I had been going to talk to you, but as you 'sucked your teeth' at me I didn't bother).

su-su /susu/   Gossip, rumours, etc.

sweet* /swiit/   (1) Pleasing, satisfying.*
(2) (Transitive verb) to please, give pleasure to.*

sweet mout'* /swiit mout/   To flatter, 'chat-up'.

tacuma(h)* /takuma/   Character in Anansi tales – in the African originals, this is Anansi's son.

tallawah* /tallawa/   (Of men) strong, reckless, stalwart.

tatta /tata/   Father, elder.

tea* /tii/   (1) Any hot, non-alcoholic beverage.
(2) (In the Caribbean) lunch.

tek* /tek/   To take. Note the following usage: **tek** dem, mek matches (make matches with them).

t'ief* /tiif/   To steal.

Tiger* /taiga/   Character in Anansi tales. Tigers, of course, are not native to Africa. However, in West African Pidgin **tiger** means a leopard.

toas(t) /tuos/   (Of a disk jockey) to add an improvisation over a reggae instrumental.

too* /tuu/   (Most often means) very. Said with a high tone when mild disapproval is indicated (Allsopp 1972).

tracing match* /triesinmach/   Quarrel.

t'row-way /trówé/   To spill.

t'row word* /truo wod/   To start a quarrel by 'passing remarks' intended to be overheard. In Black America this is 'loud-talking'.

tuku /tuku/   Thick-set person.

tuku-tuku* /túkútùkù/   Thick-set, squat.

turn, tu'n /ton/   To become: yu **turn** big woman now, since yuh a Bertie mi? (you're a grown woman now, are you, since you are calling me Bertie, i.e. first-naming me).

unu, oonu* /unu, uno/   You, your (plural). Very occasionally used for 'you' (singular) (compare US 'you-all'). Its use seems to be familiar/insulting, unlike **yu**, which can also be used for the plural.

vex, becks* /veks, beks/   Angry, annoyed.

wa mek* /wamek/   Why?

w'appen, wha' 'appen* /waapn/   A familiar greeting.

wash-belly /wash-beli/   The last child born to a mother.

wash-stone /wàsh-túòn/   A large stone in a river, like a stepping stone. Used by those who are doing their washing at the riverside.

we, weh, wa, wha* /we, wa/   What(?)

we* /we/   Who(?) Where(?)

weed* /wiid/   Marijuana.

wepart* /wepaat/   Where(?)

well done! /wel don/   So be it, that's that.

whentime /wentaim/   When(?)

who-fa /huufa/   Whose(?)

wi* /wi/
(1) We, us, our.
(2) Will as marker of future/hypothetical.
(3) With.

wikid* /wikid/
(1) English meaning.
(2) Excellent, daring.*
(3) (Rastafarian, etc.) **di wikid** means 'the police'.*

wine, wine-up* /wain, wainop/   To dance with a circling motion of the hips.

work* /wok, work/   (Can when used transitively mean) to earn. Anansi also works his plan, and works his brain.

ya* /ya/   Here.

ya so* /yá sò/   Right here.

yaa, yaw /yaa/
(1) (After a request) won't you?
(2) (After a statement) an emphatic 'you hear'.

yard* /yaad/   Home, one's house and yard: John deh a **yard** (John is at home).

yeri /yeri/   Archaic word for 'hear'; found mainly in songs and proverbs.

yeye* /yai/
(1) Eye.*
(2) (Exclamation) listen! You hear!

zomby*, jumby /zomby, jombi/   Undead, restless spirit – equivalent to **duppy** but more common in the Eastern Caribbean.

Bibliography

Abrahams, R. D. 1972: The training of the man of words in talking sweet. *Language in Society*, 1, 15–29.

Abrahams, R. D. 1976: *Talking Black*. Rowley, Mass.: Newbury House Publishers Inc.

Adams, R. 1932: *A Modern Ibo Grammar*. London: Oxford University Press.

Allsopp, R. n.d.: *Africanisms in the Idiom of Caribbean English*. Society for Caribbean Linguistics (St Augustine, Trinidad), occasional paper no. 6.

Allsopp, R. 1972: *Some Suprasegmental Features of Caribbean English and their Relevance in the Classroom*. Cave Hill: University of the West Indies.

Angelou, M. 1971: *I Know Why the Caged Bird Sings*. New York: Bantam Books.

Bagley, C. 1979: A comparative perspective on the education of Black children in Britain. *Comparative Education*, 15 (1).

Bailey, B. 1966: *Jamaican Creole Syntax*. London: Cambridge University Press.

Bailey, B. 1971: Can dialect boundaries be defined? In Hymes, D. (ed.), *The Pidginization and Creolization of Languages: Proceedings of a Conference at the University of the West Indies, Mona, Jamaica, 1968*. London: Cambridge University Press.

Barrett, L. 1968: *The Rastafarians: a Study in Messianic Cultism in Jamaica*. Puerto Rico: Institute of Caribbean Studies.

Barrett, L. 1976: *The Sun and the Drum: African Roots in Jamaican Folk Tradition*. London: Heinemann.

Barrett, L. 1977: *The Rastafarians: the Dreadlocks of Jamaica*. London: Heinemann.

Bassir, O. 1957: *An Anthology of West African Verse*. Ibadan: Ibadan University Press.

Baugh, J. n.d.: Refining historical accounts of inherent copula variation in Black English. Unpublished paper.

Beckwith, Martha. 1929: *Black Roadways: a Study of Jamaican Folk Life*. Chapel Hill, NC: University of North Carolina Press.

Bennett, L. 1966: *Jamaican Labrish*. Kingston, Jamaica: Sangster.

Berry, J. (ed.) 1976: *Bluefoot Traveller: an Anthology of West Indian Poets in Britain*. London: Limestone Publications.

Bickerton, D. 1975: *Dynamics of a Creole System*. London: Cambridge University Press.

Brathwaite, E. 1967: *Rights of Passage*. London: Oxford University Press.

Cargill, M. 1965: *Ian Fleming Introduces Jamaica*. London: A. Deutsch.

Cassidy, F. 1961: *Jamaica Talk: Three Hundred Years of the English Language in Jamaica*. London: Macmillan, for the Institute of Jamaica.

Cassidy, F. and Le Page, R. 1967: *Dictionary of Jamaican English*. London: Cambridge University Press. Revised edition, 1980.

Cashmore, E. 1979: *Rastaman: the Rastafarian Movement in England*. London: George Allen and Unwin.

Cazden, C. 1974: Play and metalinguistic awareness. *Urban Review*, 1, part 1.

Cazden, C., John, V. P. and Hymes, D. (eds) 1972: *Functions of Language in the Classroom*. New York: Teachers College Press.

Christie, P. 1979: *Assertive 'No' in Jamaican Creole*. Society for Caribbean Linguistics (St Augustine, Trinidad), occasional paper no. 10.

Coard, B. 1971: *How the West Indian Child is Made Educationally Subnormal in the British Classroom*. London: New Beacon Books.

Collymore, F. A. n.d.: *Barbadian Dialect*. Bridgetown: Advocate Co.

Crowther, Rev. S. 1852: *A Grammar and Vocabulary of the Yoruba language*. London: Sealeys.

Cruikshank, J. G. 1916: *Black Talk; Being Notes on Negro Dialect in British Guiana*. Demarara.

Crump, S. 1979: The language of West Indian school children and its relevance for schools. Unpublished MA(Ed.) thesis, Institute of Education, London.

Cundall, F. 1972: *Jamaican Proverbs*. Shannon: Irish University Press. Reprint of 1927 original.

Dalby, D. 1969: Americanisms that may have once been Africanisms. *The Times* (London), 19 July.

Dalby, D. 1970: *Black through White: Patterns of Communication*. Bloomington: University of Indiana, African Studies Program.

Dalby, D. 1972: The African element in American English. In T. Kochman (ed.), *Rappin' and Stylin' Out: Communication in Urban Black America*. Urbana: University of Illinois Press.

Dalby, D. 1977: *Language Map of Africa and the Adjacent Islands*. Provisional edn. London: International African Institute.

d'Anglejan, A. and Tucker, G. R. 1973: Sociolinguistic correlates of speech style in Quebec. In Shuy, R. and Fasold, R., *Language Attitudes: Current Trends and Perspectives*. Washington: Georgetown University Press.

Davis, S. and Simon, P. 1979: *Reggae Bloodlines*. London: Heinemann Educational.

DeCamp, D. and Hancock, I. F. 1974: *Pidgins and Creoles: Current Trends and Perspectives*. Washington: Georgetown University Press.

Dillard, J. L. 1972: *Black English: its History and Usage in United States*. New York: Random House.

Edwards, J. R. 1979: *Language and Social Disadvantage*. London: Edward Arnold.

Edwards, J., Rosberg, M. and Prime Hoy, L. 1975: Conversation in a West Indian taxi. *Language in Society*, 4 (3), 295–320.

Edwards, V. K. 1976: West Indian language and comprehension. Unpublished PhD thesis, University of Reading.

Edwards, V. K. 1979a: West Indian language, attitudes and the school. London: National Association for Multiracial Education pamphlet.

Edwards, V. K. 1979b: *The West Indian Language Issue in British Schools*. London: Routledge and Kegan Paul.

Ervin-Tripp, S. and Mitchell-Kernan, C. 1977: *Child Discourse*. New York: Academic Press Inc.

Figueroa, J. 1970: *Caribbean Voices* Vol. 2, *The Blue Horizons*. Lagos: Evans Brothers (Nigeria).

Garrison, L. 1979: *Black Youth, Rastafarianism and the Identity Crisis in Britain*. London: Afro-Caribbean Education Resources.

Gilkes, M. 1975: *Wilson Harris and the Caribbean Novel*. Kingston, Jamaica: Longman Caribbean.

Grimes, J. E. and Glock, N. 1970: A Saramaccan narrative pattern. *Language*, 46 (1).

Gumperz, J. and Hernandez-Chavez, E. 1972: Bilingualism, bidialectalism, and classroom interaction. In Cazden, C., John, V. P. and Hymes, D. (eds), *Functions of Language in the Classroom*. New York: Teachers College Press.

Hadi, S. 1977: Draft paper on linguistic diversity and the educational response (unpublished).

Herbert, C. n.d.: *In the Melting Pot*. London: ILEA English Centre.

Herskovits, M. 1941: *The Myth of the Negro Past*. New York: Harper Bros.

Holm, J. 1976: Copula variability on the Afro-American continuum. Paper presented to the conference of the Society for Caribbean linguistics on New Directions in Creole Studies, Turkeryen, Guyana.

Holm, J. 1978: The Creole English of Nicaragua's Miskito Coast: its sociolinguistic history and a comparative study of its lexicon and syntax. Unpublished PhD thesis, University of London.

Husén, T. (ed.) 1975: *Social Influences on Educational Attainment*. Paris: Organisation for Economic Co-operation and Development.

Jackson, B. 1967: *The Negro and his Folklore*. Austin: American Folklore Society.

Jekyl, W. 1966: Jamaican song and story. *The American Folklore Society*, 55. Reprinted from 1907 original.

Johnson, J. 1978: *Park Bench Blues* and *Ballad For You*, *Race Today*, January/February.

Kochman, T. 1972: Black American speech events. In Cazden, C., John, V. P. and Hymes, D. (eds), *Functions of Language in the Classroom*. New York: Teachers College Press.

Labov, W. 1966: *The Social Stratification of English in New York City*. Washington, DC: Center for Applied Linguistics.

Labov, W. 1972: *Language in the Inner City*. Oxford: Basil Blackwell.

Labov, W. and Waletzky, J. 1967: Narrative analysis. In June Helm (ed.), *Essays on the Verbal and Visual Arts*. Seattle: University of Washington Press.

Labov, W., Cohen, P., Robins, C. and Lewis, J. 1968: *A Study of the Non-Standard English of Negro and Puerto Rican Speakers in New York City: Report on Co-operative Research Project 3288*. New York: Columbia University.

Lambert, W., Hodgson, R., Gardner, R. and Fillenbaum, R. 1960: Evaluational reactions to spoken languages. *Journal of Abnormal and Social Psychology*, 60, 44–51.

Lamming, G. 1960: *The Pleasures of Exile*. London: Michael Joseph.

Lander, S. 1979: Morpho-syntactic features in the writing of second generation West Indians. Unpublished M.A. dissertation, Dept. of Language and Linguistics, University of Sheffield.

Lawton, D. 1968: The implications of tone for Jamaican Creole. *Anthropological Linguistics*, 10 (6), 22–6.

Le Page, R. B. 1972: *Sample West Indian Texts*. York: University of York, York Papers in Linguistics.

Le Page, R. B. and DeCamp, D. 1960: *Jamaican Creole: an Historical Introduction to Jamaican Creole*. London: Macmillan.

Lionnet, G. 1972: *The Seychelles*. Newton Abbot: David and Charles.

Little, A. 1975: The educational achievement of ethnic minority children in London schools. In Verma, G. and Bagley, C. (eds), *Race and Education across Cultures*. London: Heinemann.

McLeod, A. 1979: Writing, dialect and linguistic awareness. Draft paper, West Indian Writing Group, London, Institute of Education.

McNeal, J. and Rogers, M. (eds) 1971: *The Multiracial School*. Harmondsworth: Penguin.

Mercer, N. 1981: *Language in School and Community*. London: Edward Arnold.

Milner, D. 1975: *Children and Race*. Harmondsworth: Penguin.

Mitchell-Kernan, C. 1971: Language behavior in a Black urban community. Working Paper 23, University of California, Berkeley.

Moore, N. 1980: *Africa*. Bedford English Language and Resources Centre.

Morgue, E. 1957: Ashanti Story. In Bassir, O. (ed.) *An Anthology of West African Verse*. Ibadan: University Press.

NAME 1980: Draft Evidence to the Committee of Inquiry into the Education of Children from Ethnic Minority Groups (Interim Report on Pupils of West Indian origin). London: National Association for Multiracial Education.

Nettlefold, R. 1965: National identity and attitudes to race in Jamaica. *Race*, 7 (1), 59–72.

Nettlefold, R. 1970: *Mirror, Mirror: Identity, Race and Protest in Jamaica*. Kingston: Collins Sangster (Jamaica) Ltd.

O'Connor, E. n.d.: *Jamaica Child*. London: ILEA English Centre.

Ong, W., S.J. 1971: *Rhetoric, Romance and Technology*. Ithaca: Cornell University Press.

Opie, I. and Opie, P. 1977: *The Lore and Language of School Children*. London: Paladin. Paperback edition.

Ottley, C. R. 1971: *Creole Talk*. Port of Spain: Ottley in conjunction with Victory Printers.

Owens, J. 1977: *Dread*. Kingston: Sangster.

Price, R. 1976: *The Guiana Maroons*. Baltimore: Johns Hopkins University Press.

Ramchand, K. and Gray, C. 1972: *West Indian Poetry*. London: Longman Caribbean.

Reisman, K. 1970: Cultural and linguistic ambiguity in a West Indian village. In Whitten, N. and Szwed, J. (eds), *Afro-American Anthropology: Contemporary Perspectives*. New York: The Free Press.

Richmond, J. 1977: *Looking at Language at Vauxhall Manor School*. London: ILEA English Centre.

Richmond, J. 1978: *Dialect*. London: ILEA English Centre.

Richmond, J. 1979: Jennifer and 'Brixton Blues': language

alive in school. In Supplementary Reading for Block 5, PE 232 Language Development. Milton Keynes: Open University Press.

Rosen, H. and Burgess, A. 1980: *Languages and Dialects of London School Children: an Investigation*. London: Ward Lock.

Rosen, M. n.d.: Writer-in-inner-city-residence. Unpublished pamphlet, London, Institute of Education, English Dept.

Silverman, S. 1975: The learning of Black English by Puerto Ricans in New York City. In Dillard, J. (ed.), *Perspectives on Black English*. The Hague: Mouton.

Sutcliffe, D. 1978: The language of first and second generation West Indian children in Bedfordshire. Unpublished M.Ed. thesis, University of Leicester.

Sutcliffe, D. 1981: British Black English in British schools. In Mercer, E. *Language in School and Community*. London: Edward Arnold.

Sylvain, S. 1936: *Le Créole Haitien, morphologie et syntaxe*. Port-au-Prince, Haiti: Wetteren (BM ref 12911, dd 19).

Talking Blues 1976: London: Centerprise.

Taylor, D. 1977: *Languages of the West Indies*. Baltimore: Johns Hopkins Press.

Thomas, J. J. 1969: *The Theory and Practice of Creole Grammar*. London: New Beacon Books. New edition as 1869 original.

Thomas, R. 1978: Infringement and vindication. Unpublished MA (Ed.) thesis, Institute of Education, London.

Thompson, D. 1975: Children's unorganised games. *Remedial Education*, 10 (1), 8–13.

Todd, L. 1974: *Pidgins and Creoles*. Language and Society Series. London: Routledge and Kegan Paul.

Troyna, B. 1977: Angry youngsters – a response to racism in Britain. *Youth in Society*, 26, 13–15.

Trudgill, P. 1974: *Sociolinguistics*. Harmondsworth: Penguin.

Trudgill, P. 1975: *Accent, Dialect and the School*. Exploration in Language Study Series. London: Edward Arnold.

Turner, L. 1949: *Africanisms in the Gullah Dialect*. Chicago: University of Chicago Press.

Valdman, A. 1977: *Pidgin and Creole Languages*. Bloomington: Indiana University Press.

Valdman, A. 1978: *Le Créole: structure, statut et origine*. Paris: Editions Klincksieck.

Voorhoeve, J. 1962: *Sranan Syntax*. Amsterdam: North Holland Publishing Company.

Voorhoeve, J. 1971: Church Creole and pagan cult languages. In Hymes, D., *The Pidginization and Creolization of Languages*. London: Cambridge University Press.

Wagner, J. 1973: *Black Poets of the United States*. Urbana: University of Illinois Press.

Wasted Women 1973: London: Black Ink Publications.

Westermann, D. 1930: *A Study of the Ewe Language*. London: Oxford University.

Wells, J. C. 1973: *Jamaican Pronunciation in London*. Oxford: Basil Blackwell.

Welmers, C. 1971: *African Language Structures*. Berkeley: University of California Press.

Index

Survey of Linguistic Diversity in
  London Schools, 151
'syncretism', 34

Talking Blues, 63
taunting, 49, 56, 156
tense (JC verb), 99–101, 135, 137,
  141
Thomas, Rosemary, 157
Thompson, Dorothea, 48–9
toasting, 49, 57
Togo, 45, 62
tone,
  Bajan, 139
  JC, 110–12, 120, 127
Trinidad, 5
  dialect continuum, 138
  folklore, 35, 37
  French Creoles, 5, 37, 41, 44, 142
  literature, 59
  proverbs, 41, 44, 45
  riddle, 47
Troyna, B., 155
Trudgill, Peter, 126
Tshiluba, 39
Tucker, G. R., 76
Twi, 34, 104, 111

unemployment, *see* employment
United States, *see* America

Valdman, A., 15n
value system, conflicting, 54, 58, 157
verbal art/performance, 10, 35, 45, 49,
  52, 54, 55, 57, 66, 156–7, 172

verb system,
  aspect, 8–9, 99–101
  copulas, 101–2
  negative, 99
  pre-verbal markers, 9, 100
  progressive verb markers, 126–7
  repetition, 104–5
  serial verb chain, 103–4, 134
  stem forms, 98–9
  tense, 8–9, 99–101
vocabulary, 13–16, 34, 40, 174–95
voice overlap, 66
Volta, 43
Voorhoeve, J., 19
vowels,
  Bajan, 139–40
  JC, 22, 105–7

Wagner, J., 20, 65
West Africa, *see* Africa
West Indies, *see* Caribbean, Jamaica,
  Trinidad, *etc.*
Wheatley, John, 20
Wheatley, Phillis, 20
'winding', 48
Windward Islands, 5
Wolof, 32
'woofing', 56, 156
word order, 17–18, 102, 119
work song (jamma), 21

Yoruba, 32, 139
  proverbs, 42, 44
  serial verb chain, 103
  tone, 111

Zaire, 39